EMERGENCY MANAGEMENT EXERCISES

FROM RESPONSE TO RECOVERY
Everything you need to know to design a great exercise

By **Regina Phelps**, RN BSN MPA CEM
President and Founder Emergency Management & Safety Solutions Inc.

Chandi Media

www.ChandiMedia.com

260 Whitney Street
San Francisco, CA 94131

415-643-4300 (voice)
415-643-4621 (fax)

EMERGENCY MANAGEMENT EXERCISES
FROM RESPONSE TO RECOVERY
Everything you need to know to design a great exercise

Published by:

Chandi Media
260 Whitney Street
San Francisco, CA 94131
415-643-4300 (voice)
415-643-4621 (fax)
www.ChandiMedia.com
Info@ChandiMedia.com

ISBN: 978-0-9831143-0-7
LCCN: 2010940162

Contents

Acknowledgements and thanks

Life is, indeed, a journey and not a destination, and writing is a bit like a journey as well. This journey began in the early 1980's when I started EMS Solutions and began to study this concept of exercise design. I started out by taking FEMA classes and attending the California Specialized Training Institute (CSTI) in San Luis Obispo. And now, many years later, I have designed thousands of exercises and through that tool, have been able to help hundreds of organizations.

I am thankful to my many clients around the world who have trusted me with their information, and even more importantly, with their employees and executives who participated in the magic that we have weaved over these many years and exercises. I am very thankful that they allowed me to design experiences that helped to transform them and ultimately helped them to achieve their company and personal preparedness goals.

I am deeply indebted to my editor, Meg Keehan, who has perfected crawling into the deep recesses of my brain (sounds icky, doesn't it?) and is always able to translate exactly what I am saying into meaningful sentences, and who has helped to enrich our exercises and this book in ways I can't fully imagine. Thank you, Meg!

I am also very thankful to my assistant, Carol Taylor, who keeps my office and life running smoothly while I am traveling hither and yon around the world conducting these exercises. Without Carol keeping everything running, I wouldn't be able to be on-site delivering these experiences. Thank you, Carol, for all that you do for me.

And lastly, I am very thankful to my mom, Dollie Phelps, who was a very successful entrepreneur, civic leader, and an incredible role model to me. She could never exactly describe what I do for a living to anyone, but she was always proud of my achievements. Thanks Mom – I miss you.

I have taken my brain and poured it into these pages. I hope you find it helpful. Let me know how you are doing.

— Regina Phelps

Regina@ems-solutionsinc.com

Preface

Why write a book on how to conduct emergency management exercises? That's a great question that I have debated myself for some time.

Let me answer the question by telling you about my background. I have been in the field of emergency management since 1982, conducting over 100 exercises a year for many years. Most of these exercises are functional exercises (see Chapters 2 and 14), and are often for large, complex companies.

What I have observed in my years of professional practice is that although many companies hold exercises, and the organizers may be emergency response subject matter experts, they do not excel in the discipline of conducting the actual exercise. Which means they simply don't get the best results out of their effort.

What I've learned from doing so many exercises for so many years is that with a bit of careful planning, creativity, and vision, you can develop a great exercise that will really help build your response plan, program, and the response team.

Helping you build your plan, program, and team is what this book is all about.

Thanks for reading!

— Regina Phelps
CEM, RN, BSN, MPA

CHAPTER 1
Why conduct emergency management exercises?

Exercise benefits

If you have elected to read this book, I am probably already preaching to the choir. However, it is very likely you may need to convince your organization's management, your colleagues, or your boss as to why you should conduct an emergency management exercise. So what are the benefits of an exercise program? Let me count the ways... there are at least nine of them!

1. Evaluate communication between different groups.
2. Assess the allocation of resources and manpower.
3. Assess the adequacy of current procedures and policies.
4. Determine overlaps and holes in planning.
5. Clarify roles and responsibilities.
6. Improve individual performance.
7. Motivate employees.
8. Build confidence.
9. Increase general awareness of proficiencies, deficiencies, and gaps.

Evaluate communication between different groups

In an exercise, you can really determine if you have properly connected the communication dots. Have you linked up everyone that needs to communicate with each other? Have you discovered the correct communication nodes in your teams and within the organization? What communication tools work the best to connect these dots? The protocol, the tools, and the people can all be exercised to make sure your plans, processes, and communications are clear and well documented.

Assess the allocation of resources and manpower

Have you allocated enough people for the response and recovery effort? Do you have enough resources (tools, locations, money) to make it all work when you need it to? An exercise can allow you to examine the resources you have earmarked and determine if you might have too little, too much, or just the right amount for what you are trying to achieve.

Assess the adequacy of current procedures and policies

Exercises are a great place to find out if procedures really work. A person who intimately knows the job or document will often not be able to see what is missing or isn't clear when asked to do a review. But give that same plan to someone who doesn't do that job routinely and ask him or her to do the task or the procedure – that's where you'll learn a lot.

Many organizations believe that they can design policies "on the fly" when the need arises. However, in an exercise they often learn how hard that is to do that with everything else going on at the same time. They often leave the exercise experience with a new-found understanding that policies developed in advance can be a better product, a huge timesaver, and can reduce stress as well. Many companies experienced this first-hand during the first few weeks of the H1N1 outbreak in the spring of 2009. They had failed to develop specific policies on such issues as compensation, use of masks, and how to handle employees who come to work sick. Many were scrambling under pressure to figure it out.

Determine overlaps and holes in planning

Plans are written in a vacuum and often seem "fine" when viewed from a normal, business-as-usual situation. It is only when you attempt to use something – like a plan – that you see if it really works or not. Exercises give people an opportunity to use the documents they wrote while thinking "this is never going to happen" – until, of course, it does!

Clarify roles and responsibilities

Plans are often written using many assumptions throughout their development. Ah, the word *assumption*! This one single word can get us into a lot of trouble in our daily life, and even more so in the field of emergency management. *Assuming* what someone's role is, *assuming* what action should be done, *assuming* who has responsibility for something – that's when we can get into real trouble.

An exercise can help validate and clarify who is doing what, when, and where, by putting the team into the situation, which will raise many, if not all, of those assumptions to the surface. They can then be addressed and – hopefully – taken care of before the next exercise or a real event takes place.

Improve individual and team performance

There is nothing like practice to really make a difference in improving the performance of both the individual and the team. Think back to the first time you drove a stick-shift automobile – you had to think through every single motion: Push in the clutch, edge it out just a bit, give the car a little gas. Too much or too little of one or the other made for a jerky ride. But reflect on how you perform that same action now – it takes no thought at all, no consternation. You've developed "muscle memory," and simply drive effortlessly and with a smooth gliding action. That is what we want for our teams when disaster strikes, and exercises will help them develop that "muscle memory" by providing a means to practice, practice, practice.

Motivate employees

Do you ever have a hard time getting your employees to delve into their business continuity plans or practice a recovery action? When someone knows an exercise is coming up, it is human nature to brush up on the required knowledge and skills. When management is playing in an exercise, it also helps to motivate people to review their plans and processes well in advance. After all, no one wants to look bad in front of his or her boss!

Build confidence

We want our teams to be confident when disaster strikes. We want them to move forward executing on their plans. If the plan doesn't work or needs modification, we want to teach them in advance that they have the confidence to make corrections and keep moving forward. An exercise helps stretch and build that confidence muscle, and do it in a safe environment.

Increase general awareness of proficiencies, deficiencies, and gaps

Lastly, by its very nature, an exercise will help you really understand the maturation level of your program, plan, and teams. At the end of a well-designed exercise, you have a very good idea of where your holes, gaps, and deficiencies are lurking, as well as your strengths and assets.

Exercise outcomes

When your management team asks you, "So, what are we going to get out of doing an exercise?" what can you tell them? The outcome of an exercise program is four-fold:

1. Improve overall company readiness.
2. Improve the emergency management system within the company.
3. Provide individual training.
4. Facilitate updating a plan to be current and up-to-date.

Improve overall company readiness

There are only two ways to know if your plans are going to work. One way is to have a disaster and just see how it goes. The second is to conduct an exercise. It makes sense that the preferred method would be the latter, not the former. It is a lot more effective to have an exercise to determine how and if your plans will work – and it's a lot less stressful! You also get to go back and change the plans without the pain of going through a real disaster.

Improve the emergency management system within the company

Every exercise improves your overall emergency management system. It will point out areas for improvement in the four key areas of any emergency management system: Mitigation, preparedness, response and recovery.

Provide individual training

As we all know, adults learn best by doing, not by reading a book or reviewing a plan. If you want your folks to know what to do when disaster strikes, you need to practice it in advance and actually "live" the experience.

Facilitate updating a plan to be current and up-to-date

The overall goal of an exercise is to wind up with an up-to-date plan. Once an exercise has concluded, you will know the areas of the plan that need to be modified and improved. The revisions that occur after every exercise continue to refine the plan and keep it "battle ready."

What is an exercise?

So then, what is this thing that is better than sliced bread? What is an exercise? An exercise is the performance of duties, tasks, and operations in a way very similar to the way they would be performed in a real emergency. Very simply put, an exercise is an activity that is designed to promote emergency and business preparedness. I always tell people, imagine that this is a movie, a play, or a book. We are creating a "reality" and then placing people into that reality and observing how they perform.

How often do you need to conduct an exercise?

The general rule is twice a year, unless your organization has a lot of activations (situations where the emergency management team comes together in response to a real event). Even if that is the case, then you still need one formal exercise per year to ensure learnings from real activations get included into the plan, processes, and policies, as well as to allow practice without the stress of a real event hovering over the team members' heads.

Thankfully, most private sector companies have relatively few plan activations. On the flip side, that means that there is a lot of planning for an infrequent happening (thank goodness!), which also means that the exercise program provides the team with the only chance they have to practice their plan and processes. My experience has demonstrated that the team will be pretty green for their first few exercises. But around exercise number three (provided the team remains relatively stable from exercise to exercise), they really begin to gel as a team and the plan has been shaken out fairly well. As the old proverb goes, "Practice makes perfect."

Terminology

Do you remember the childhood rhyme, *"Sticks and Stones"?* It goes like this:

> *Sticks and stones*
> *May break my bones*
> *But words will never hurt me.*

While that may be true, it is also true that words can influence behavior. Notice that I have not used the word "test" anywhere in this text. That is **totally** on purpose. When you hear the word "test," what immediately comes to your mind? For many people, the first word out of their mouth after hearing "test" is "grades"! And for many of us, the opportunity to pass, fail, or to otherwise be judged might not be a pleasant experience.

Exercises are stressful in their own right. We want people to make mistakes – in fact, we encourage it. Calling an exercise a "test" implies potential punitive action and a judgment being passed on the participant's performance. To that end, I discourage the use of the word "test" because words do influence behavior – and sometimes not for the best.

Summary

Regular exercises provide us the best opportunity to know if our plans are complete, and if staff is ready for the disasters and emergencies that are likely to befall our organizations.

CHAPTER 2

The six types of exercises

Before we dive in...

Before we begin a discussion about the types of exercises, it is important to ask an important question: "What kind of plan are you exercising?" It's important to identify what you are exercising before you begin designing the exercise.

It may sound obvious, but many designers are not clear about the answer to that simple question when they start planning. And if you're not clear about what kind of plan you are exercising, you can get into trouble very quickly. The answer to the question will drive many facets of the exercise, such as the number of people involved and how complicated the exercise is. In particular, for this chapter, the answer will also determine the "starting time" of the exercise narrative (see Chapter 5).

Emergency management

Let's first look at the term "Emergency Management." What does it mean? While there are many different definitions of Emergency Management, a good, broad explanation is that it is the "organization and management of resources and responsibilities for dealing with all aspects of emergencies, including mitigation, preparedness, response and recovery." That's a very broad definition, encompassing a lot of moving parts.

Since the term "Emergency Management" is so broad, then, you need to know where you want to focus. You will probably be concentrating on one of three areas:

▶ Emergency response
▶ Business continuity
▶ Disaster recovery

Emergency response plan exercises

An emergency response exercise deals with the immediate response activities that are required from "hour zero" of the incident until the initial life safety issues have been resolved. For example, if you want to do an earthquake emergency response exercise, you would start the "exercise clock" immediately after the earthquake stopped shaking. If you were conducting a tornado exercise, the clock could start right after the twister hits your building. The emphasis of these types of exercises are on life safety, immediate damage assessment, and working with local emergency responders.

Business continuity plan exercises

An exercise that is focused on business continuity will be timed to begin after the immediate life safety and emergency response activities have concluded. Think about it – if you are doing an earthquake exercise, and you set the "exercise clock" to begin the moment after the earthquake hits, your staff would likely be more worried about life safety and emergency response issues, NOT business continuity. If you don't think about this carefully, you would start that exercise and be sorely disappointed when the team was more concerned with accounting for staff and treating injuries than restarting the business.

Disaster recovery plan exercises

The traditional definition of disaster recovery is the recovery of technology, such as a data center or corporate telephony. These exercises are traditionally a full-scale exercise with an actual "field response" where teams actually go to the hot site to restore systems. These teams typically go to the hot site as soon as it is feasible to do so, so the "exercise clock" starts after the initial life safety issues have been resolved.

Six types of exercises

Once you've determined what you are exercising, there are six types of exercises to consider:

1. Orientation (including workshops and training)
2. Drill

3. Tabletop (including Basic and Advanced)
4. Functional
5. Full-scale
6. Multi-site

Each style of exercise will be discussed in this chapter. Subsequent chapters will detail how to actually run most of these exercises, and will include sample agendas, exercise timelines, and exercise plans.

Please keep in mind that team or plan development is an evolutionary activity. The normal progression is to start your team's development with an Orientation exercise, then progress to a Tabletop, then onto a Functional exercise, and then perhaps a Full-scale. This is an opportunity to watch your team to mature, with each step along the way deformed to build their skills and confidence. Don't try to progress your team to quickly or they may lose confidence and you will lose credibility.

Orientation exercise

Orientation exercises are great ways to introduce a new team to a plan or a new plan to a team. It uses a simple narrative and is delivered in a PowerPoint or other visual slide format in a conversational, non-threatening manner. This style exercise is useful in the following situations to orient:

▶ A new Incident Management Team (IMT) to their role.
▶ An Executive Management Team (EMT) to their role.
▶ A business unit or a recovery team to their new Business Continuity Plan (BCP).
▶ A facilities and security team to their company responder role.
▶ A disaster recovery (DR) team (technology team) to their plan in prep-

Orientation exercise characteristics

— Introduces the participants to plans and procedures
— Introduces a new plan or a revised old one
— Requires no previous experience
— Helps orient new staff or leadership

Planning cycle: About one month
Exercise time: From 1 to 2 hours

aration for a full-scale DR exercise.

Orientation exercises are known for their simplicity and ease of time in preparation. It should take you less than a month to plan this style of exercise. The actual exercise time is usually from one to two hours.

Workshops and training

Although you can hold workshops and training for your emergency teams separate from an Orientation exercise, I tend to approach them as part of the orientation experience as it seems logical to combine them.

Imagine that you are introducing a new plan or process to a team or group, or perhaps the team itself is brand new. A combination experience – where the first part of the activity is a training and/or workshop about the material, and the second part is the Orientation exercise – allows you to first teach them the material and then immediately apply their new learning by doing a simple (yet effective) exercise. This really helps them integrate and reinforce the material, and provides a much better platform to assimilate the information.

Drill exercise

You have likely been doing Drills for a long time. Don't believe me? Think back – remember your first fire drill in elementary school? It was the test of a single emergency response function – how to respond to a fire – in other words, a Drill exercise.

Drills are relatively simple exercises to plan. Since they involve the performance of one skill, the planning and execution is pretty straightforward.

Drill exercise characteristics

— Tests a single emergency response function
— Involves actual field response
— Provides practice or test under realistic conditions
— Involves all levels of responders

Planning cycle: About one month

Exercise time: Between 10 and 60 minutes

What type of drills might you do? Here is a list of the most common:

▶ Fire drill
▶ Radio drill

▶ Tornado drill
▶ Earthquake drill (drop & cover)
▶ Shelter-in-place drill:
  ▷ Weather
  ▷ Violence
  ▷ Hazardous materials

Due to the relatively simple nature of a drill exercise, this style will not have its own chapter.

Tabletop exercise

Tabletop exercises are by far the most common and frequently performed exercise. There are essentially two versions:

▶ Basic: Seeks to solve problems in a group setting via discussion and brainstorming.

▶ Advanced: Includes the introduction of inputs and an exercise Simulation Team acting as proxies for the outside world.

Tabletop exercise characteristics

— Provides a more realistic and more stressful atmosphere than previously mentioned exercises

— Presents a simple narrative.

— Includes injects to the exercise (usually; see below)

Planning cycle: About two months

Exercise time: At least three hours

Basic tabletop

A Basic Tabletop starts with a simple exercise plan and straightforward narrative. The team responds to the challenge in a discussion format; in other words, they tell the Facilitator "this is what I would do to solve the problem." It is a step up from an Orientation exercise but remains conversational.

Advanced tabletop

The idea of an Advanced Tabletop came about in the late 1990's when we were doing a lot of Y2K exercises. One of the things I kept seeing was how teams would solve problems during exercises. They would be presented with a situation and a series of assumptions, and were asked to come up with a solution. In most cases, the team members would snap their fingers and – amazingly! – they always got what they wanted. They were not dealing with potential real problems, such as not having enough equipment, running out of diesel fuel or water, not getting staff where they needed them – whatever! I realized that the teams would not be able to build a solid plan if they were never challenged to, so I introduced the concept of a Simulation Team into the experience (see Chapter 10).

In an Advanced Tabletop exercise, a small Simulation Team of two to four people portray various members of the "outside world," such as "Emergency Responders," "Media," "Contractors/Vendors," or my favorite, "Genius-of-all-Trades" (who are Sim Team members who can play anybody).[1]

The wonderful thing about the Simulation Team is that they provide "push back" to the exercise player. When the player says, "I need 100 laptops now," the Simulator can say, "I am sorry, I can't get you 100 laptops now; I can get you 50 today and the other 50 next week." This makes the player look closely at their plans and figure out how they can make do until those other 50 laptops arrive. Through the Sim Team, you have succeeded in making them really have to work through their plan.

Functional exercise

Functional exercises are fully simulated and feel very realistic. To be "fully simulated" means that participants perform all activities (within the confines of the Emergency Operations Center [EOC]), and all exercise injects are delivered by a Simulator or an audio-visual tool (see Chapter 6). In a Functional exercise, the team would order a resource, but wouldn't deploy them. During a Functional exercise, you could walk into an EOC and within a few moments swear that this event was really happening. I spend most of my time doing Functional exer-

---

1   I used to call this role "Jack-" or "Jill-of-all-Trades. However, as a Mac user since 1984, in recent years, I changed it to "Genius-of-all-Trades," in deference to Apple and their "Geniuses," brilliant folks who can answer any tech problem.

cises – they are fun to design and a hoot to facilitate and deliver.

In this type of exercise, the exercise players are presented with a full exercise plan and a detailed narrative. There are a significant number of injects delivered by the Simulation Team to provide that realistic give-and-take that makes the event seem real. This exercise also has a larger cast of characters on the

Functional exercise characteristics
— Simulates a more complex narrative
— Requires participants to perform the activities
— Involves more participants including Simulators, controllers/evaluators, observers, and bigger design team
— Introduces sophisticated inputs and other media

Planning cycle: About two to three months

Exercise time: At least four hours

day of the event: more Simulators, Controllers/Evaluators, Observers and a bigger Design Team. This exercise is also more equipment-intense, with all injects being delivered by phone or other technological means.

Full-scale exercise

The final exercise is a Full-scale exercise. This has all of the complexity of the Functional exercise, with the added layer of an actual field response on top. In a Full-scale exercise, you order a resource AND you deploy it. These exercises are more commonly done in the public sector, such as an airport exercise that simulates a crash (with

Full-scale exercise characteristics
— Involves field response (actual mobilization of field personnel and resources, and the actual movement of emergency response teams, equipment, and resources)
— Presents the events in real time, is complex and detailed
— Requires a rigid time schedule, which adds to the stress level
— Is more expensive

Planning cycle: About four months (minimum)

Exercise time: Four to eight hours

actual "victims" being removed from the tarmac), or a terrorist exercise (for example, with Sarin gas "victims" being treated at the scene of a Federal building). Some private sector organizations located in a seismic environment may do a Full-scale exercise that simulates the triage and treatment of earthquake "victims," sets up a first-aid station, then rolls up to the formation of their EOC.

These exercises are expensive to plan and deliver, and are very time-consuming. Those organizations likely to do a Full-scale exercise are those with major regional risks, such as hurricanes and earthquakes. One Full-scale exercise commonly done in the private sector is a disaster recovery exercise where the technology teams go to the company's actual hot site and perform a real recovery of tapes and data. Due to the infrequent nature and the complexity of the Full-scale exercise, this style will not have its own chapter.

Multi-site exercise

Multi-site exercises are a great way to exercise regional disaster response plans or to practice how one team would support another. If you have an Incident Management Team located at headquarters and part of their mandate is to support the recovery of mission-critical locations, one way to exercise this responsibility is to have an "affected site" reach out to the headquarters team during an exercise, and then both teams work together to practice their roles and communication linkages.

Multi-site exercise characteristics
- Involves one or more locations.
- s either a Functional or Full-scale style exercise
- Assesses communication, hand-offs between teams, and a team's ability to support another team
- Is complex in design, administration, and facilitation

Planning cycle: About six months
Exercise time: Half-day to full-day

These exercises are expensive to plan and facilitate, and are very time-consuming. Those organizations likely to do a multi-site exercise are those with major regional risks (such as hurricanes and earthquakes), multiple locations, and/or companies whose recovery strategy is to transfer processing to another site. The best way to know if this will work is to do it. Due to the highly specialized and complex nature of the multi-site exercise, this style will not have its own chapter.

Comparison of the three most common exercise styles

	ORIENTATION	TABLETOP	FUNCTIONAL
Participant experience level	Beginners; this may be their first exercise	Have had some prior exercise experience	Experienced players
Style	Casual, very conversational	Group discussion, led by the Facilitator	Highly interactive; Simulators deliver exercise injects and the players respond in real time
Degree of realism	Lacks realism	Lacks realism	Feels like "the real deal," but does not deploy resources
Exercise tone	Non-threatening	A little stressful for players; a little performance anxiety	Lifelike, stressful for the players
Design team?	Usually not needed	Yes	Yes
Participants	Facilitator, exercise players	Facilitator, exercise players. May have Evaluators and Simulators	Facilitator, exercise players, Evaluators, Simulators. May have Controllers
Leader	Facilitator	Facilitator	Facilitator. In larger exercises, a Controller.
Location	EOC or conference room	EOC or conference room	EOC
Equipment deployed?	No	No	No
Complexity	Easy to plan, usually less than a month	Planning time usually around two months	Planning time usually two to three months
Average exercise length	One to two hours	At least three hours	At least four hours, often all day
Evaluation	Participant evaluation, Facilitator observations	Participant evaluation, Facilitator and Evaluators' observations	Participant evaluation, Facilitator and Evaluators' observations
Cost	Relatively inexpensive	Modest expense	Moderate to high expense

Summary

Exercises are an evolutionary activity, starting with the basic Orientation exercise and moving along the exercise continuum to an Advanced tabletop or Full-scale exercise. It is important to select the appropriate exercise for the maturity level of the team and the plan being exercised. A desirable goal of any exercise is for the team members to reflect on the experience and say "we learned a lot, found some gaps, and continued to make progress."

CHAPTER 3

The design team:
Your secret weapon in exercise design

Why you need a Design Team

Many emergency management professionals tell me that they design their exercises by themselves. I can't imagine that. I don't care how smart you are, how long you have been at the organization, or how many exercises you have done in the past, you can't know or think of everything. In my opinion, the best exercises use a Design Team. What makes an exercise hit home and really sizzle is a tailored narrative and highly specific injects. You can't do that alone; you need some help. Your Design Team has two main jobs, to validate the narrative, and to develop the injects.

It also turns out that in addition to helping you validate the narrative and developing the injects, though, there are great side benefits to having a Design Team:

▶ It is a great way to bring more people into the fold, to bring them into your program. The Design Team members become believers, and they share their belief with others.

▶ The Design Team learns so much when they are involved in designing an exercise. They learn about the strengths and weaknesses of the processes and the plans.

▶ The insight that the Design Team gains by being part of the exercise design process can help build awareness in their sphere of influence, along with engaging and exciting others to make the plans and the program better.

Who should be on the Design Team?

A top-notch Design Team member will have several qualities:

▶ A good basic knowledge of the overall business.

▶ At least a year or more with the company in order to know some of the ins and outs of the place.

▶ A subject matter expert (SME) in an area you will likely be touching on in the narrative. A typical Design Team will include members from the following departments:

   ▷ Facilities (critical if doing a "hard"[2] incident).

   ▷ IT (essential if impacting any technology).

   ▷ Security (often knows lots of interesting tidbits).

   ▷ Human Resources (especially if there are lots of "human capital" issues).

   ▷ Representatives from the affected key departments or key lines of business (to help you develop highly specific injects).

Note that the departments listed above are *typical* to Design Teams. Your organization may benefit from having team members representing a different 'slice' of your business.

Let me give you an example to illustrate why it's important to have all the right players. I once did an exercise where the client wanted the exercise narrative to be a fire. I told him thought that wasn't an effective narrative; after all, they were in a contemporary high-rise building with full sprinkler fire protection. He still was very keen on having a fire. After pondering a bit, I suggested we first introduce a water main failure. This would disrupt water delivery to the building for 24 hours while it was being repaired. Then, the fire could occur, maybe even be considered "suspicious."

I asked the client if the building had a fire cistern (fire cisterns are a reliable year-'round water source for fire-fighting efforts, and is a common high-rise back-up water supply for just such an occasion). When he said "no," I insisted we get a Facilities person on the Design Team to validate that, plus other building assumptions we were making. Sure enough, our Facilities rep confirmed they had a cistern with 25,000 gallons of water available at a moment's notice. By calling in additional "brain power" to the design process, we

---

2   A hard incident is a event with a physical impact – something you can see or feel. A fire, earthquake, tornado, or hurricane are all examples of hard incidents.

learned that a fire scenario simply wouldn't have worked for this exercise.

This is a good example of why you need a Design Team, and who to consider to be part of that team. If you launch a narrative or insert an inject into your exercise that is incorrect or poorly vetted, your exercise can go flat and you lose credibility. The players will wave off the incorrect information or the inject; too many "wrong" pieces of information and eventually the exercise is over in their minds, probably before the actual end of the exercise. Your Design Team will help ensure that the information is correct and spot on.

What makes a good exercise Design Team member?

As you are reading this section, you are probably already getting an idea of who would make a good team member. I often find that people who like this kind of thing enjoy being on the team and will often sign up repeatedly and help design many exercises. When picking Design Team members, look for the following skills:

- ▶ Creative.
- ▶ Meets or exceeds deadlines.
- ▶ Detail-oriented.
- ▶ Can think on their own.
- ▶ Can keep a secret.
- ▶ Are not on the exercise team.

Creative

Creative people are open to ideas and can really play off the ideas of others. These are folks who can see all colors of the rainbow versus those who can only see black and white. When an idea gets launched in a team meeting, even if it's a bit different or "hasn't happened before," these are the folks who take the idea and run with it, often coming up with a new twist or angle to a problem.

Meets or exceeds deadlines

Design team members need to meet or exceed their research or homework deadlines. One person who lags behind can drag down the whole group and slow your design process to a crawl. Your Design Team members need to work well under pressure and keep on schedule and on track.

Detail-oriented

The design process involves coordinating a lot of information, often down to a very detailed level ("How many gallons of fuel are left in the generator?"). Your team needs to uncover what those details are and research their ramifications within the framework of the exercise. Very often, these details hold the keys to the success of your exercise.

Can think on their own (no 'yes men' [or women], please!)

I want people on my team who will question the direction the exercise is going and push back if it doesn't seem to work. Do you remember the concept of "groupthink"? "Groupthink" is a term coined by social psychologist Irving Janis in 1972 after studying historical events, including Pearl Harbor and the Bay of Pigs. The "groupthink" phenomenon occurs when a group makes faulty decisions due to group pressures. These pressures lead to a deterioration of "mental efficiency, reality testing, and moral judgment."[3] Members essentially try to minimize conflict and reach consensus without critically testing, analyzing, and evaluating each others' ideas. Although it isn't always easy to hear, some of my best design team members are the ones who will say to me "that's a bad idea," or "this won't work, here's why." Those people are invaluable to your design effort.

Can keep a secret

For most exercises, the exercise narrative is not divulged in advance, therefore, secrecy is a critical element of in the design process. Remember – our Design Team knows all, therefore, they need to be good at keeping exercise specifics to themselves. Team members need to be discreet when conducting their research. Trench coats and surreptitiousness are encouraged! We all know people who can't keep their mouths shut – we don't want those folks on our team.

Are not on the Exercise Team

It should go without saying that our designers can't be a player on the day

3   Janis, Irving L. (1972). *Victims of Groupthink*. New York: Houghton Mifflin.

of the exercise. They know everything and it is usually very hard for them then to react to the narrative on exercise day as if they were learning about it for the first time. If one of your best design people *must* also be playing in the exercise, find other ways to get the information you need from their brain. One way might be to schedule time to interview that person individually and ask them a series of questions that go in many directions, but not involve them in the Design Team meetings. This way, you can get a lot of data that you'll need, and, if you've asked wide-ranging questions, they really can't tell what scenario will be put to them during the exercise.

How many do you need?

Good question! How many Design Team members do you need? To address the core areas mentioned earlier, you will generally have between 5 and 7 individuals, although depending on the situation, sometimes the group may be larger. The largest design team I have ever managed was a 50-person team designing a Y2K exercise for a global financial institution – that was a bit like managing a global circus!

Design Team time commitment

It is always good to set expectations when soliciting Design Team members and let them know how much time this will take. Here is a rough time estimate to consider:

Attending all Design Team meetings: Usually 90 minutes to two hours each. There could be three to five of these depending on the length and complexity of the exercise.

Completing homework for each meeting: Usually 30 minutes to one hour per homework assignment.

One more possible role for your Design Team members to play

If you are using a Simulation Team (see Chapter 10) in your exercise, I find that Design Team members usually make great Simulators. They know the exercise intimately and are already a cohesive team. If you plan to ask them to be Simulators as part of their design job, in the interest of fair disclosure regarding the time commitment for this process, be sure to include that task when you ask for their participation. Additional time commitment for your Designer-turned-Simulator (approximate):

Simulation Team orientation – 90 minutes to two hours (usually a few days before the exercise).

Exercise day – However long you have scheduled the exercise.

Design Team member checklist

List the subject matter areas you need in the Design Team, brainstorm possible names, and then contact them to secure their commitment to participate.

SUBJECT MATTER AREA	POSSIBLE NAME	CONTACT INFO	COMMITMENT YES/NO
Facilities			
Security			
Technology			
Human Resources			
Communication			
Key departments or lines of business			
Other area			
Other area			
Other area			
Other area			
Other area			

Summary

Your Design Team is critical to your exercise. Selecting the right team members will make your exercise credible, exact, and challenging. It will also engage more people in your program, and help to build a culture of awareness and support for your program.

CHAPTER 4

Your roadmap – the exercise plan

The big question

There is one question you want to ask yourself, your colleagues, your design team, and others over and over again during the design process. This question will help you stay on track and on vision from start to finish: *Why are we doing this exercise?* Don't be turned off by the simplicity of that question, the answer holds the key to your exercise.

I started asking this simple question when I noticed how easy it was for people to get caught up in the excitement of the design. The team would be so fully engaged in the process that the next thing you know, we had Martians[4] landing in the middle of the exercise (as a metaphor, of course), and we were adding things that didn't meet the mission. Or perhaps someone has a deliverable – or even a covert agenda – and they want to see if the exercise can deliver on it. If you're not alert, they can insert something into the exercise that is, again, off-mission. Be alert, and keep asking *Why are we doing this exercise?* to avoid filling your exercise with things that don't meet your objectives and can end up derailing the experience.

After one such exercise that seemed to deteriorate into a participant's personal agenda, I came up with the idea of asking *Why are we doing this exercise?* as a regular part of the planning process. When it seems like the exercise is heading in the wrong direction, or the group's enthusiasm is taking us into fun – but not necessarily helpful – territory, or I question someone's agenda, I just ask the simple question, *Why are we doing this exercise?* The discussion that inevitably follows helps to realign the energy and makes sure we are delivering

---

4   The War of the Worlds was an episode of the Mercury Theater on the Air. It was performed on October 30, 1938, aired over the CBS radio network and directed and narrated by Orson Wells. The episode was an adaptation of H.G Wells' novel The War of the Worlds, and so many people believed it was real that it created pandemonium around the country. http//en.wikipedia/wiki/The_War_of_the_Worlds_%28radio

on the exercise objectives.

When embarking on the design process, this simple question can also help you:

- ▶ Determine what type of exercise will likely deliver the best results.
- ▶ Develop the exercise goal, scope, and objectives.
- ▶ Assist you in determining which narrative will yield those results.
- ▶ Keep you and the design team on track.

Now that is a pretty handy question to ask!

Exercise type

What type of exercise are you creating? I always ask myself three questions to help me decide which type is the best:

- ▶ The first question is always *Why are we doing this?*
- ▶ Second question: What is the maturity of the program and the plan?
- ▶ Third question: What is the experience level of the team being exercised?

Once you have the answer to those questions, you should be able to determine which exercise type will yield the best results:

- ▶ Orientation.
- ▶ Drill.
- ▶ Tabletop (Basic or Advanced).
- ▶ Functional.
- ▶ Full-scale.
- ▶ Multi-site.

Exercise scope

The scope of the exercise quickly tells you who is participating in the exercise and who is not. The exercise scope consists of, but is not limited, to the following:

- ▶ The locations and sites will be participating in the exercise.
  - ▷ Geographical area.
  - ▷ Included business units or departments.
- ▶ The participants.
  - ▷ Those actually "playing" in the exercise.

▷ Those who will be simulated.

▶ The groups/departments at risk or in flux that would benefit from the experience.

　　▷ Any areas/plans/groups you are concerned about.

　　▷ Any recent changes in people, plans, processes, or equipment that pose new issues.

　　▷ Any known weaknesses you wish to explore, such as new plans or no plans at all, new staff, or uninterested managers.

▶ Other areas or items that should be considered when determining the scope:

　　▷ Off-hours: Are evening or weekend exercises in play or are they off-limits?

　　▷ Will you have shift changes? (Usually included in longer exercises.)

　　▷ Will this be a "surprise" exercise, where the team players don't know they will be 'activated'?

Defining the type and the scope of the exercise helps determine your staffing requirements for the exercise. This includes the number of design team members, simulators, and observer/evaluators that you will need.

Exercise scope – sample wording

Here are some examples of exercise scope statements:

▶ "This exercise includes the activation of the Corporate Incident Management Team; all other groups and departments are simulated."

▶ "The North American teams are activated; all other company locations around the world are simulated."

▶ "The data center is activated; all other departments are simulated."

▶ "The Corporate Headquarters Incident Management Team, the London IMT, and the Bangalore IMT are activated; all other departments and company locations are simulated."

Exercise goal

The exercise goal is the defined purpose of the exercise, answering our now-favorite question *Why are we doing this exercise?* The goal is an umbrella statement that gets back to the heart of the exercise and really does answer the *Why are we doing this exercise?* question. As an exercise designer, I find that I refer back to the goal over and over again to help keep the design team – and me – on track.

What is a goal? It is a brief and clearly stated aim of what you want the exercise to accomplish. Combined with the exercise objectives, the goal drives the exercise design, and keeps you on track to achieve the results you are seeking out of the experience.

Goals are developed by discovering what the key players want to get out of the exercise experience through a series of interviews or conversations. Here is a list of people that I normally like to chat with to develop the exercise goal:

▶ Incident Commander.

▶ Business continuity manager.

▶ Key business unit manager.

▶ Key executives.

▶ Other key department managers such as Facilities, Security, Technology, Human Resources, and Communications.

I find that it doesn't take asking a lot of questions to find out what people what to get out of the exercise; in fact, many times, I only need to ask one or two to learn everything I need. Here is my short list:

▶ What are you looking to achieve in the next exercise?

▶ Have you had any recent incidents or plan activations? If yes, please tell me about them.

▶ Are there any departments or groups that you are concerned about? If so, who are they and why are you concerned?

▶ How would you evaluate the overall readiness of the organization?

▶ When you are laying in bed at night, are there any things that keep you awake? In other words, have you ever heard yourself say to yourself, "if (fill in the blank) happens, we are in real trouble"? Tell me what that is.

Exercise goal – sample wording

Here are some examples of exercise goal statements:

▶ "Assess the ability of the Crisis Management Team to manage a regional event."

▶ "Assess the emergency response aspects of the company plan and overall team readiness."

▶ "Experience a global pandemic event that impacts the company and its staff, and assess the company readiness."

▶ "Experience an event that impacts the Denver office and surrounding area, and assess the ability of the team to manage the event."

Exercise agenda

Don't forget to "plot out" your time for the exercise day. You may be estimating that your exercise "playtime" will be for 2 hours, but your exercise participants will be with you longer than that. ("Playtime" is the time the participants will be actively engaged in the narrative.) Develop an agenda and socialize it to make sure all players know what the time commitment will be.

Exercise duration

Talking about an agenda naturally leads to another fairly basic question: How long should the actual exercise playtime be? Your exercise can be conducted over a half- or full-day format, but that usually includes introductions, plan review, debriefings, and other "non-play" activities. In terms of actual playtime, how long should the players be "playing" before there is a break/meal or a change in the story (such as advancing the exercise time clock)? The following questions are some things to consider when building your agenda and thinking about how long the players will be actually engaged in "playing."

Should you have a "play" time of less than 2 hours?

Your answer to the big question (*Why are we doing this exercise?*) will determine if a shorter playtime will be effective. Be aware that it's hard to get a lot of issues raised and problems resolved in such a shorter amount of time. In addition, with a short exercise, human nature comes into play. Participants know they only have a short period of time to "work the issues," so they drag their feet and don't resolve an issue because they know time will run out soon. In addition, the story and the issues raised in the narrative and injects will not have time to evolve and develop.

I have seen exercises where every 15 or 30 minutes the clock advances, and more and very different issues are introduced each time. This structure never allows the participants the chance to solve any "meaty" issues or deeply work through any problem, which likely means the plans will be very shallow in their design – nothing gets a deep workout.

Should you have a "play" time of longer than 2 hours?

Again, what is your answer to the big question, *Why are we doing this exercise?* If the answer is "to wear the participants out," then yes, you will need a longer "play" time. Or if your answer is "to challenge the team and address issues that have been glossed over or forgotten," then, yes again, a longer play time is called for.

As it turns out, most learning occurs in 2- to 4-hour chunks of time; after that, players get tired and distracted, and the activity needs to shift somehow. Break up the playtime with a lunch break, clock shift, team turnover, or other means to provide participants a way to recharge.

What are the pros and cons of having a half-day or a full-day exercise?

These will still depend on your answer to the *Why are we doing this exercise?* question, but the following information may also be helpful:

- ▶ Half-day session:
  - ▷ It is easier to get on team participants' calendars.
  - ▷ It requires a shorter planning cycle.
  - ▷ It takes less time, resources, and energy.
- ▶ Full-day session:
  - ▷ It provides the ability to take the learnings of the morning and adjust plans/actions in the afternoon. This can be very powerful, as participants leave the experience feeling that they have made great progress. If you are doing a half-day exercise and the team didn't feel good about their performance in the morning, they may leave the experience feeling a bit deflated. If you are doing a second exercise in the afternoon, the extra time allows them to modify their processes and improve their play, thereby feeling much

better about themselves, the plan, and the team when they leave.

▷ It provides an opportunity to "move the clock forward" from a few hours to several days later in the second exercise. This gives you the chance to look at issues regarding a sustained operation.

▷ It can provide an opportunity to practice a shift change, where "Team A" has to turn over status and information to "Team B," further addressing issues that may arise in a sustained operation.

Sample agendas for different exercise types

A clearly written agenda helps keep everyone on track and sets expectations for the exercise players, simulators and evaluators. The following are some samples for you to consider.

ORIENTATION EXERCISE AGENDA

ACTIVITY	TIME	DISCUSSION LDR
Coffee	8:30 AM to 9:00 AM	
Introductions, goals, objectives	9:00 AM to 9:15 AM	S. Executive
Review plan (This could be a BCP, department plan, or Incident Managememt Team plan)	9:15 AM to 10:15 AM	D. Continuity
Orientation exercise	10:15 AM to 11:30 AM	R. Facilitator
Exercise debrief. Complete participant evaluations.	11:30 AM to Noon	R. Facilitator D. Continuity

TABLETOP OR FUNCTIONAL EXERCISE HALF-DAY AGENDA

ACTIVITY	TIME	DISCUSSION LDR
Coffee	8:30 AM to 9:00 AM	
Introductions, goals, objectives, exercise briefing	9:00 AM to 9:30 AM	S. Executive
Exercise	9:30 AM to 11:30 AM	R. Facilitator
Short break to grab lunch	11:30 AM to 11:45 AM	
Over lunch: Exercise debrief. Complete participant evaluations.	11:45 AM to 1:00 PM	S. Executive

TABLETOP OR FUNCTIONAL EXERCISE FULL-DAY AGENDA		
ACTIVITY	TIME	DISCUSSION LDR
Coffee	8:30 AM to 9:00 AM	
Introductions, goals, objectives, exercise briefing	9:00 AM to 9:30 AM	S. Executive D. Continuity
Exercise #1	9:30 AM to 11:30 AM	R. Facilitator
Executive briefing #1	11:30 AM to 11:45 AM	Incident Commander
Debrief of Exercise #1 (over lunch)	11:45 AM to 12:30 PM	R. Facilitator
Plan revisions	12:30 PM to 1:00 PM	Teams
Exercise #2	1:00 PM to 3:00 PM	R. Facilitator
Executive briefing #2	3:00 to 3:15	Incident Commander
Press conference	3:15 to 3:30	Communications team
Break	3:30 to 3:45	
Debrief of Exercise #2. Debrief of overall experience. Complete participant evaluations.	3:45 to 4:20	R. Facilitator
Next steps and thanks	4:20 to 4:30	D. Continuity

Exercise objectives

What is an exercise objective? An objective is essentially a sub-goal. It identifies a short-term, measurable step that is moving toward achieving the overall exercise goal. I develop exercise objectives in two ways:

▶ In your initial interviews, the answer to "what do you want to get out of the exercise?" is a great place to start. You will learn what is important and where there are likely to be issues to explore.

▶ Go back to the basic question – *Why are you doing this exercise?* It will shed light on the exercise objectives and give you a wealth of information.

The many benefits of exercise objectives

Objectives are like touchstones. You will find yourself going back to them again and again through the entire design process.   It is important to spend the time to develop and validate them.

Guide the design

Objectives are used to guide the design and to assess the outcome. Well-written objectives will narrow and hone the scope of the exercise plan. Does the narrative meet all of your expected outcomes? Go back and look at the objectives. When you want to make sure you are still on track, go back to the objectives. When are you trying to assess whether or not your have a complete set of injects, go back to the objectives. They are the guiding light of the design process.

Provide direction for the exercise narrative

Objectives really establish the direction of the exercise. A well-written set of objectives will always point you to the best narrative to achieve them. Objectives also help to keep the exercise and the players on track.

Frame exercise injects

The objectives control the direction and type of exercise injects. For example, if one of your objectives is about communications (employee, client, media, etc.), then you will likely have several injects that push communication issues from those entities.

Provide context to evaluate the exercise

Lastly, objectives are used to evaluate the exercise. When you assess the exercise, look to the objectives to see if each of them were achieved.

How many objectives do you need?

There is no set number of objectives that you need to have. Ideally, you should have the number necessary to address the issues you are trying to raise and assess in the exercise. Most exercises will have between 3 and 5 overall general objectives. There may also be additional sub-objectives for a specific team, a department, or location.

Characteristics of good objectives

Writing good objectives takes a bit of practice. Your objectives should be clear and easily understandable. A well-written objective should be:

▶ Simple.

▶ Concise.

▶ Measurable (when possible).

▶ Achievable.

▶ Realistic and challenging.

A strong objective details what behavior is expected from the player to demonstrate that he or she can perform the skill or task. In particular, well-written objectives use strong action verbs to describe that behavior. "Action verbs" are verbs that specifically describe what the subject of the objective is doing. They are observable and better communicate the intent of what is to be completed.

These types of verbs carry a great deal of information in a sentence; they can also convey emotion and a sense of purpose that extends beyond the literal meanings of the words. Here are some action verbs:

Advise	Consult	Install	Negotiate	Sponsor
Apply	Contrast	Instruct	Orient	Supervise
Assemble	Demonstrate	Interview	Persuade	Teach
Assess	Develop	Investigate	Plan	Train
Brief	Facilitate	List	Produce	Tutor
Communicate	Identify	Manage	Recite	Write
Compare	Influence	Mentor	Revise	
Conduct	Initiate	Motivate	Select	

SMART objectives

"SMART" is an acronym to assist you in writing strong objectives.[5] It is a catchy little saying that touches on the specific qualities you want to see in well-written objectives. The objectives should be:

▶ Specific – Explicit, with a key result. It should be clear about what, where, when, and how the situation will be changed.

▶ Measurable – Clear as to whether you are meeting the objective or not,

---

5   In researching the origin of SMART objectives, there is no one clear author for the concept although it is in *"Leadership and the One Minute Manager: Increasing Effectiveness Through Situational Leadership"*, Ken Blanchard, Patricia Zigarmi, Drea Zigarmi, William Morrow, 1999

and quantify the targets and benefits.

▶ **A**chievable – Attainable.

▶ **R**ealistic – Practical enough to be met, especially within the confines of an exercise time limit.

▶ **T**ime bound – State the time period in which it will be accomplished.

Exercise objectives – sample wording

1. "Orient new team members to their roles and responsibilities."
2. "Orient new team leaders to their roles on the Incident Management Team."

3. "Assess the ability of the team to develop the company message, and produce the following communication materials: employee communications via SMS and email, web page update, the client message, the social media messages (Twitter and Facebook), and a press release."
4. "Assess the team's ability to conduct a senior management briefing."
5. "Assess the ability of the Incident Commander and designated Team Leaders to conduct a timely Incident Action Planning meeting and develop a written IAP."
6. "Assess the ability of the Planning & Intelligence team to review the business continuity plans and determine a recovery strategy for the businesses that meet the recovery time objectives."
7. "Assess the ability of the Operations team to communicate the technology recovery status in real time during the exercise."

Participant instructions

This section of the exercise plan tells the exercise players what they can expect from the exercise and what is expected of them during the exercise. It really gives you, the designer, a chance to communicate your thoughts and intentions, and introduce what might be some new concepts to the players.

"Stay in role"

One important concept to communicate in the instructions is the expectation that the players will "stay in role" the entire time. That simply means we don't want them talking about what they did last weekend or the television show they watched last night. We want them to be in the here and now, to act and believe that this incident has really happened. When done this way, after a short period of time, the mind can't tell the difference of what is real from what is imagined. We want them to feel as if this incident/experience has really happened; if they are chatting about the baseball game last night, it takes away from the "reality" of the experience.

> *"What is real? How do you define real? If you're talking about what you can hear, what you can smell, taste and feel, then real is simply electrical signals interpreted by your brain."*
> —*Laurence Fishburne* as *Morpheus from The Matrix*[6]

Expect mistakes

Problems, issues, and mistakes in an exercise are a good thing. An overarching goal of any exercise is to find out what doesn't work. Some people are very concerned about their performance and about making mistakes. You need to reassure them that making mistakes is a healthy outcome of any exercise, and that exercises are not a "fault-finding activity." There is no grade issued at the end of the experience. There will likely be a lot of mistakes – and that is a good thing!

Embrace "Exercise Magic"

I created the term "exercise magic" some years ago to explain some of the exercise creativity we use to create the narrative, the story, the scene, and the experience. For example, how did this team just "magically" come together? How is it that you learned about this narrative as you did? Whatever their question is, I ask players to not get hung up in how things have happened. We have simply used a bit of "exercise magic" to create this event. If we somehow missed the mark, don't get hung up, don't fight the narrative, and please don't say "This could never happen." We ask the players not to debate that something has hap-

---

6   *The Matrix* is a 1999 American science fiction-action film written and directed by Larry and Andy Wachowski.

pened, could have happened, or is happening – just accept that it is!

"Time-outs"

Just as with small children, there is occasionally a need to take a "time out." There are two primary reasons to take a time out.

1. *If a real emergency happens.* It is important that you let everyone know what you will do in the case that a real emergency happens in the middle of your exercise – obviously, the exercise stops and the incident is assessed and managed. If it is a small issue, such as a false fire alarm, you may be able to get back to your exercise. If it's a bona fide emergency, then the team gets to "practice" for real.

2. *If the team is so off track that you can't "right them" any other way.* In my many years of practice, I have only had this happen once. The team had so wrapped themselves around a proverbial axle that the only way to unwrap them was to announce a "time out" and set the record straight. Better to do that than to have them off-base the entire time.

Don't be afraid to use a "time out" if that what it would take to get the exercise back on track. The simplest way to do a time out is to simply stand in the middle of the exercise space/room and with a loud outdoor voice call out to everyone, "Excuse, me; excuse me. I need to make an announcement." And then simply correct whatever issue needs to be corrected or state whatever needs to be stated. Then simply thank them and tell them, "the exercise has now resumed – carry on!"

Participant instructions – sample wording

1. "Exercises have the greatest value if they are treated as real. Please stay in role the entire time."

2. "Don't just think about responding to what is coming at you – remember to keep one eye into the future and play the game of 'what-if.'"

3. "As the exercise progresses, details may not be as complete as you would like. The value is in the process, the dialogue, and the experience. The design team has worked to make the situations as realistic as possible – if we have somehow missed the mark, please don't let that

hang you up."

4. "You may only use what is in place as of today; if new equipment is being added next month, it is not in place and can't be used."

5. "Exercises are for learning; we expect mistakes. The goal is to develop the team and the plan, and to learn from the experience."

6. "In order to make this exercise work and to facilitate the learning process, a certain amount of 'exercise magic' has been used. We ask you not to debate that something has happened, could have happened, or is happening – it just is!"

7. "Questions regarding the exercise should be directed to the exercise facilitator."

Communications

The communications section of the exercise plan tells the players everything they need to know about exercise communication. This section details:

▶ Who it is appropriate for them to communicate with and who it is not.

▶ What your expectations are for communications. In an Advanced Tabletop, Functional or Full-scale exercise, players should simulate all communications that they would do in a real incident using the Simulation Team or whomever else you allow them to call.

▶ If using a Simulation Team, describe who they are and how to use them.

▶ If using a Simulation Team and phones, detail how to use the phone directory.

Communication instructions – sample wording

1. "A Simulation Team will act as the 'outside world' for this exercise. All problems must be solved by calling the Simulation Team, acting as proxies for the outside world. This includes any call that you would make to find out information, order equipment, etc.

2. "Simulators will answer the phone, "May I help you?" Just tell them who you are looking for and magically they will turn into that person."

3. "If you need to find out 'real information' (a fact) from an employee or department, you may call them directly. Tell them you are in an exer-

cise (without the details) and need information to answer a question or resolve a problem."

4. "The 'genius-of-all-trades' can be anyone you need them to be."

5. "All information in the narrative and that provided by the facilitators and simulation team is to be considered valid."

6. "However, just like in a real disaster, messages can be jumbled, and rumors can start on incorrect information or assumptions. Multiple versions of the same problem may occur."

Evaluation

One of the last sections of the Exercise Plan is the discussion on how the exercise will be evaluated. In this short section, you simply state the different methods you are using to evaluate the exercise. (The actual evaluation process is discussed in Chapters 9 and 10.)

Evaluation section – sample wording

▶ "The exercise will be evaluated by use of participant written evaluations, the debrief session, and the facilitator and evaluators' observations based on the objectives."

Narrative

The last section of the Exercise Plan is the narrative, or storyline, of the exercise. This is an important part of your plan, so it gets its own chapter; see Chapter 5.

Summary

The Exercise Plan is the foundation for the exercise experience. It is important that you carefully construct this document and have it completed and approved before the first Design Team meeting. Look at it as your roadmap with all of the rules of the road carefully laid out for all to review – and agree to – before the exercise begins.

CHAPTER 5

The real story:
The development of the exercise narrative

The last portion of the exercise plan is the narrative or exercise scenario. This is comprised of three parts:

1. Artificialities.
2. Assumptions.
3. Narrative/scenario.

Artificialities

"Artificialities" is an odd word isn't it? It is word that describes all of the things that are blatantly "pretend" for the exercise, and are obviously not true. You can look at the exercise artificialities as things that would improve your exercise if you could simply change them. They include such items as:

▶ Changes to date and/or time.
▶ Changes to equipment.
▶ Changes to a location.
▶ Changes to weather.
▶ People who are unavailable.
▶ Conditions necessary to conduct the exercise.

This is one of the great things about an exercise – you can do anything you like! You are creating the reality that your players will have to operate in. You can be king or queen of your exercise world!

Changes to date and/or time

The date or time is one of the most common things to modify. During your design process, find out the dates and times that have a great impact on the organization, and make a decision to move the scenario if it makes sense for the maturation of the team. Some examples:

▶ If the date of your exercise is August 15, but having the exercise occur during a heavy processing period would make it much more challenging for the business, it might be a good idea to move the date to July 28 (for example), smack dab in the middle of month-, quarter-, or year-end preparations.

▶ If the trading desk closes at noon, but your exercise begins at 1:00 PM, you might consider changing the exercise time to 9:00 or 10:00 AM.

▶ Perhaps your real exercise date is on a Friday. From the perspective of what you want to achieve in the exercise, that would give your team the entire weekend to recover – probably without having to worry about many employees – which probably wouldn't stretch them that much. So maybe pretending it's a Monday or a Tuesday makes the team deal with the critical, immediate issues.

Changes to equipment

Perhaps you want a piece of equipment to be available, but in the "real world" it isn't available for another 30 days – state in your artificialities that it's available. Or vice versa, you could specify that something is unavailable when it really is, such as a diesel generator that just happens to be "completely torn apart for its annual service" on the day your power outage scenario occurs… Because coincidences like that never happen. Right?

Changes to a location

What do you do if you narrative makes your headquarters building unavailable, but that happens to be where you are holding the exercise? In that case, your artificialities would state where the Emergency Operations Center (EOC) is meeting for the purposes of the narrative. A statement such as "The EOC is meeting at the Hilton Hotel, which is the back-up EOC location" will do the trick.

Changes to weather

Why would your artificialities call for an unseasonable heat wave, cold snap, heavy rains, an ice storm, or other severe weather situations? Maybe your team has gotten a bit complacent over the years and you want to challenge them to handle employees who are "out on the street." Or you want the team to deal with other aspects of their recovery planning. Changing the weather can present additional challenges that the current weather might not. If it's appropriate for the location, you could "make" the following weather happen:

- ▶ Tornado – "The spring weather has been unseasonably warm and sultry over the past few days. A tornado watch has been issued for the county until 5:00 PM tonight."

- ▶ Flooding – "There has been 4" of rain over the past 12 hours, with more forecast for the next 24 hours. The National Weather Service issued flash-flood warnings until 7:00 AM tomorrow."

- ▶ Severe winter weather – "Since midnight, over 8 inches of snow have fallen. As of 6:00 AM, the temperature has dropped to 28 degrees Fahrenheit. More snow is forecast for today starting at noon."

People who are unavailable

One of the great fallacies of a response situation like the one you are developing is believing that all of your staff will be able to show up after any disaster. I hear this belief from clients all the time: "Oh yes, everyone here is dedicated and will do whatever they can to get to work to help recover the business."

After the Northridge earthquake in Los Angeles (1994), there were many managers who were surprised when between 25 and 40% of their staff didn't come in. People will care for their families, their loved ones, and their homes first. Then they'll come in to work, if it's possible. Depending on the event, 20%, 30%, 40% - or more – will not be able to come to work for whatever reason. How can you accommodate this statistic in an exercise?

Well, you could simply present a percentage of employees that can't come in as an artificiality: "Thirty-seven percent of your staff is not able to reach the office." That presents a number, but it isn't very meaningful. Which 37%? You know the team will decide that the 37% are staff they don't need for the recovery.

There are several ways to make it more personal and make them think about how to handle back-up personnel:

- ▶ Specify certain letters of the alphabet are unavailable. State that the people whose last names begin with that letter are unable to come to work. If you use this method, maximize its impact by spending careful time selecting strategically valuable letters – in other words, pick letters of employees who are considered critical to the enterprise. "The employees whose last names begin with the letters B, G, M, and T are not available at all" works just fine, especially if Sue **B**illings and Joe **M**anager are the "go-to" people who know "everything."

▶ Identify key people. Many organizations have a few people who are priceless to the company. They know how to get everything done and they know all the key contacts. Often, that information is only in their heads – nothing is documented. For the purpose of your exercise, why not send them on a well-needed vacation and make them unreachable for a week or two? Perhaps they are salmon fishing in Alaska, taking a cruise in the Mediterranean, or bird-watching in Bhutan. "John Lewis and Barbara Charters are on vacation in Bali for two weeks and are totally unreachable" should make your team figure out how to get things done in their absence.

▶ Injure – or kill – specific staff. Your exercise could specify that a particular employee (a real – named – employee, not a made-up person) has been injured or killed in the incident. Obviously, this may not work for every company; some organizations do not have the appetite for this type of situation. However, if you can manage it, it is a valuable technique. The situation could be created via an artificiality of the exercise plan, or as an exercise inject. How do you approach "injuring" or "killing" someone? This may need a little "kid glove" handling, but my personal practice is not to ask permission to injure someone, but always ask if you can "kill" them in the exercise. He or she might find it a bit alarming to have a co-worker issue condolences to them a few days after the exercise – wouldn't that be bad form?

▷ As a side note, you notice that I am referring to a real person. Why use a real name? The name of a real employee creates a sense of authenticity and immediacy. Stating that "Nina Summers died in the fire" usually sends a collective chill across the room and instills a real deep sense of reality. A fake name could never do that.

Conditions necessary to conduct the exercise

Your exercise may require certain conditions in order for it to work; you need to include those in the exercise plan. While these may often be weather-related variables (see above), there may be other situations you need to manufacture. You may want events such as a power outage that calls for the company to rely on its generator, or a "brown-out" situation where the local power company has issued a request to decrease power usage during peak times. Or perhaps you may want a major water main break in front of your office where the water company reports it will be 48 hours before repairs are complete. If this is the case, be sure to spell out the situation.

Assumptions

It is human nature to make assumptions. If you want to make sure that people are forming the assumptions you want them to make, and not make up their own assumptions, you need to clearly state what you want them to assume. If you don't tell them what to assume, participants often will come up with their own assumptions, creating their own internal information – which may not be in line with what you want them to assume. If your assumptions and their assumptions aren't the same, the end result can be a derailed exercise.

When you clearly lay out the ground rules and tell people what they can assume (and sometimes what they can't assume), you are less likely to have conflict in the course of the exercise. Here are some situations you might want to consider addressing in your assumptions section:

- ▶ After an earthquake, they might wonder when help is arriving, what is happening to the phones, or who is coming to work.
  - ▷ "The city will be isolated for 24 hours."
  - ▷ "The telephone systems are operating normally."
  - ▷ "All critical employees who are supposed to come to work have shown up."
- ▶ After a power outage:
  - ▷ "The diesel generator turned on immediately after the power outage and is running normally."
  - ▷ "Traders were able to execute their trades as normal."

▶ After a fire:
  ▷ "Authorities have ordered city buses to the area to begin to move people away from the fire."
  ▷ "Emergency responders are caring for injuries at the entrance to the train station."

Narrative/Scenario

The narrative prepares participants for the exercise experience. It is the overview of the event. I like to think about it as the beginning of the movie. The narrative describes the environment at the time the exercise begins, and provides all of the necessary background information in order to get started.

Most people often begin the design process with the narrative – they dive right in to what the story is. I usually end the design process with the narrative. I believe the exercise plan should be well-developed before you decide on the narrative. That puts you in the position to select the best story to meet the needs of the exercise.

Whenever you are deciding on an appropriate narrative, the first question I ask is whether it's a "hard" incident or a "soft" incident.

"Hard" incident

A hard incident is probably what most people think of when they are designing an exercise. This is one you can tangibly see and feel; in other words, an event where there is a physical impact. Fires, earthquakes, floods, tornadoes, hurricanes, mudslides, violence at work – these situations all produce a physical, tangible result, a hard incident.

"Soft" incident

So then a "soft" incident the opposite of a "hard" incident? In some ways the answer is 'yes.' Soft incidents are those more insidious events that (usually) leave no physical evidence behind. What comes to mind when I say that? How about a product recall? A major product failure? A computer virus or someone hacking into the credit card file? The meltdown of the financial markets?

All of those incidents would be considered soft incidents – there is no physical damage, but the brand and reputational impacts to the organization are huge.

Think of the incidents faced by the following companies and consider your reactions to them: Toyota, Johnson & Johnson, Firestone, British Petroleum (BP), Goldman Sachs. Each of those companies have experienced an incident(s) that impacted their reputation and brand. Some handled them very well; others could have done better. These soft incidents also make great exercise narratives.

Narrative ideas

A great source of narrative ideas is the hazard risk assessment of your location. Here are the some of topics to consider when picking a narrative.

Natural hazards

▶ Earthquake.
▶ Volcano.
▶ Tidal wave/tsunami.
▶ Wildfires.
▶ Hurricanes.
▶ Storm surge.
▶ Tidal flooding.
  ▷ Weather:
  ▷ Tornado.
  ▷ Flood.
  ▷ Winter storms (snow, ice storms).
  ▷ Lightning.
  ▷ Mudslides.
  ▷ Wind damage.
  ▷ Solar storms.

Your buildings' neighbors (one-mile radius)

▶ Train tracks (especially those used for freight).
▶ Freeways.

- ▶ Manufacturing plants.
- ▶ Government buildings, consulates, embassies.
- ▶ High-profile buildings.
- ▶ Controversial companies.
- ▶ Natural gas or product pipelines.
- ▶ Construction work.
- ▶ Special events in your city (e.g., the G-20 conference, a visit of the Queen of England).

Your buildings' neighbors (50-mile radius)

- ▶ Military base (within 10 miles).
- ▶ Airport (within 10 miles).
- ▶ Nuclear power plant (within 50 miles).
- ▶ Dam (within 50 miles).

Human risks

- ▶ Terrorism (think B-NICE):
  - ▷ Biological.
  - ▷ Nuclear.
  - ▷ Incendiary.
  - ▷ Chemical.
  - ▷ Explosive.
- ▶ Mail contamination (such as anthrax).
- ▶ Bomb threats or blasts.
- ▶ Workplace violence.
- ▶ Robbery, thefts.
- ▶ Labor disputes, strikes.
- ▶ Sabotage:
  - ▷ Cyber-sabotage.
  - ▷ Product tampering.
- ▶ Kidnapping, extortion.
- ▶ Embezzlement, fraud.

Infrastructure failures (regional)

▶ Power outages (localized or grid failure).

▶ Water main breaks.

▶ Fiber cuts.

▶ Road or bridge failures:

▶ Sinkholes.

▶ Bridge collapse.

Infrastructure failures (your facility)

▶ Pipe break.

▶ Roof collapse.

Environmental and health risks

▶ Asbestos.

▶ PCBs (polychlorinated biphenyls).

▶ Poor indoor air quality (IAQ).

▶ Toxic mold.

▶ "Sick building" syndrome.

▶ Hazardous material spill.

▶ Community health risks:

   ▷ SARS.

   ▷ Tuberculosis.

   ▷ Influenza A pandemic.

   ▷ MRSA (Methicillin-resistant Staphylococcus aureus).

Geo/political risks

▶ Political environment.

▶ Social environment.

▶ Economic environment.

▶ Human rights.

▶ Brand protection, trademark issues.

▶ Counterfeiting.

Other areas of risk

Review the following documents for ideas that will be of particular interest to you:

▶ Business Impact Analysis. Are there any concerns in the BIA?
▶ Critical department BCPs. Are there areas of weakness that could be further exposed and then resolved?
▶ Emergency response plans.
▶ Crisis communications plans.
▶ Data recovery plans. Technology failures could be the central focus of the narrative, or could be an interesting "sidebar" issue.
  ▷ Computer virus.
  ▷ Denial of service attack.
  ▷ Network(s) or server(s) failure.
  ▷ Hot site unavailable.
  ▷ Software error.
  ▷ Service provider failure.
  ▷ Hackers.

When all else fails, read the news! One of the best places for exercise ideas is a newspaper or online news site. There are stories every day of events that you could use as your narrative.

Narrative flow

Once you have selected a narrative, you need to consider the flow of the event or incident.

▶ Was there a build-up to this event? Did your event just "happen," like a fire? Or was there a build-up, for example, like a hurricane (a hurricane watch is issued, then a hurricane warning, and finally the hurricane hits)?
▶ Did the event just happen or is it already in progress? Remember back to Chapter 2, if you start the clock soon after the event begins, you are designing an exercise that is life-safety and emergency-response focused. If you want more of a business continuity focus, you need to start the exercise clock a bit later so most life safety issues can be resolved.

▶ How did you find out about it? What is/was the discovery mechanism? For example, if this is a workplace violence narrative, did you find out because gunfire was heard and then the exercise begins? Or perhaps the police have already arrived on the scene and apprehended the perpetrator.

▶ What details (such as time, location, extent of damage) do you need to present at which point? What information is going to be included as background information in the exercise plan, and what information will be delivered into the exercise via exercise injects?

▶ What is the sequence of events? Plot out the flow of the exercise. What is in the baseline narrative? What is added in the exercise injects? It is important that you – the designer – are clear about the sequence, as you hold the vision for the exercise. It must be crystal clear to you.

▶ Do you have initial damage reports? If so, is any of that information included in the narrative? Where are you going to include details about the exterior and interior of the building, equipment, the overall condition of the facility, and other key parts to your story?

Finally...

The last item to consider is an important one: Is your narrative realistic? While it is possible that commercial planes can be hijacked and sent into buildings, and large iconic financial behemoths can actually fail, you may want to consider a less extreme scenario for your exercise. It is important to really ask this hard question throughout the design process. Your design team can validate the facts of how the event would play out, but you are ultimately responsible for ensuring that the baseline story meets the "smell test" of realism.

Keeping the exercise plan under wraps

One of the things I am often asked is whether I give the players the complete exercise plan in advance of the exercise. In other words, should they know the story before they arrive? As a general rule, no, I don't hand out the exercise plan in advance – however, there are always exceptions. Why would you share the story line ahead of time? What are the benefits to doing that?

What are the disadvantages? The answers touch on three areas:

▶ The duration of the narrative.

▶ The complexity of the exercise.

▶ The culture of your organization.

When deciding if you should make the storyline known before the exercise, this should be just another one of those many times that you ask yourself the question, *Why are we doing this exercise?*

Duration of the narrative

If the exercise narrative represents a sustained operation – in other words, it's been "going on for a few days" – I would very likely give the players the exercise plan at least 24 hours in advance. Why?

I'll answer that with an example: Imagine you're working with an earthquake narrative where the "exercise clock" starts at 72 hours post-earthquake. It's very likely that the exercise plan would have several pages of detailed background information, such as information about the impact around the region, what has happened at the organization, and the overall recovery status of the area and the company. That's a lot of information to absorb and integrate in just a relatively few minutes before the start of the exercise.

In addition, in this situation, had the earthquake been real, the players would already have been thinking intensively about these problems for the past 72 hours, not just five minutes. It would be unrealistic – not to mention unfair – to drop it on them and then say, "Go!"

Complexity of the exercise

Some exercises are highly detailed and complex; it's difficult to absorb all the information and then start acting in role. As an example, I have conducted numerous exercises with utility companies. They normally have incredibly complex data available on the issues leading up to a failure – detailed grid conditions, specific equipment issues, impacts to personnel, and conditions across the state. As with a sustained operation, the depth of the data is so great that for the players to really be able to meet the objective and benefit from the exercise, they need to know the narrative in advance to absorb the information and begin to process it.

Culture of your organization

There are some organizations that really struggle culturally with not having the opportunity to pore over the plan in advance. In my experience, this seems to occur primarily in what I would call a "cerebral culture," in an organization that spends its time deep in thought, research, deliberation, and debate. The debate and validation of the narrative is often exceedingly important to many of the players, and it is difficult from them to move forward if they disagree with a point or comment. In situations such as this, it is often not worth withholding the information from them. Although I have found that situation primarily occurs primarily in academics, it also shows up in other fields as well.

Summary

The narrative is the last piece of the puzzle in the exercise plan. Take your time to select a narrative that will best meet your objectives and deliver on the question *Why are we doing this exercise?* Once you have selected the narrative, carefully conduct the due diligence to ensure that it is fully vetted, is realistic, and hits "on all cylinders."

CHAPTER 6

The drivers – exercise injects

Once the exercise begins, how do you move the story forward and ensure that your objectives are reached or that you've motivated certain behaviors? Welcome to the exercise inject.

What exercise types use injects?

Of the five exercise types, three make use of injects:

▶ Tabletop (Basic or Advanced).

▶ Functional.

▶ Full-scale.

What are exercise injects?

An inject is simply a pre-scripted message that is provided to players during the course of an exercise, with "message" being defined liberally (see "Exercise Inject Delivery Methods" below). Injects continue the story that began with the baseline narrative you gave the team at the start of the exercise. Think about it from this perspective: you are creating the story, the movie, or the television show, and in the narrative of the exercise plan, you've only told them how it begins. If you don't tell them something has changed or the situation has progressed, how else would they know? This is your reality, and you need to continue to pull them into the story by introducing new information, plot changes, or themes.

What is the purpose of an exercise inject?

In addition to providing more information about how the story is progressing, most exercise injects are meant to ask the recipient **to do something**. After all, the exercise is about working towards the exercise objectives and ultimately achieving the goal of the exercise. That requires the players to respond, to act, or to do something; therefore, most injects will have one or more questions to be answered or issues to be resolved. Some injects, however, may simply provide additional background information regarding the storyline, or they may act as additional data or "FYI" to the players relating to an issue or situation.

Other than purely "FYI" injects (which should be a very small percentage of your total injects), injects should influence action among the participants in at least one of four ways:

▶ Decide.
▶ Validate.
▶ Consider.
▶ Defer.

Decide

Exercises are an action-oriented activity. Many injects will likely require the players to make a decision about something they should be doing.

Validate

Injects may require players to gather information, and find out more data so that an issue can be validated. They can then determine if further action should occur, and, possibly, what that action should be.

Consider

Sometimes an inject will require players to discuss, deliberate, and/or consult with others. These could be people inside their own team, on other teams, or perhaps the Simulation Team. A well-framed inject is a great way to determine interdependencies, and also to ensure that you have identified the right players for the team.

Defer

Not everything is critical. Not everything requires immediate action. Giving players injects that require them to evaluate the inject and then place it on a priority list for later action is a helpful experience. Often giving them lower-level issues or low-priority problems to handle is a good training tool, as humans have a tendency to work on everything that is presented to them. Providing some items that don't need immediate attention helps players establish priorities.

Exercise inject characteristics

Exercise injects are really the "drivers" of the exercise and can have a mix of several characteristics:

▶ Point to the objectives.
▶ Describe a situation.
▶ Stimulate action.
▶ Expose unresolved issues.
▶ Escalate an issue.

Point to the objectives

Injects generally point towards the objectives. This goes back to the discussion on exercise objectives (Chapter 4) and how important they are. As you design the injects, you should always have your eye on the objectives. What are you trying to achieve in this exercise?

For example, if you have an objective regarding communications (i.e., developing media messages, employee, or client communications), you need injects that require that type of response. This means you will likely have injects with queries from the media, clients, and employees – all of which require some type of communication response.

Describe a situation

After the baseline narrative has been reviewed at the start of the exercise, how do the players know that anything has happened or that there has been a change to the story? Along with expecting the team to do something, an inject can provide new material and new information for the teams. These injects continue to describe the disaster incident, environment, and/or situation.

Stimulate action

The overriding priority of most injects is action. The goal of an inject is to stimulate the participants to action and get them to do something!

Expose unresolved issues

Any issue that is either unresolved or not handled adequately can be rein-troduced via an ad hoc inject. Your observers/evaluators/controllers (those people who are observing the action for you) can help you identify which is-sues have been unresolved and which the Simulation Team should re-address. Or your observers can take a more active role, and keep the unresolved in-jects alive by asking the players about them until they have been addressed to completion.

Escalate an issue

An inject can also escalate an initial or primary problem from the narra-tive, creating secondary or tertiary problems. For example, in an earthquake scenario, consider the following:

- ▶ **Primary event:** The earthquake scenario, as described at the begin-ning of the exercise.
- ▶ **Secondary event:** Once the earthquake scenario has been described, an inject can raise a secondary event, such as a building collapse.
- ▶ **Tertiary event:**   After the building collapse inject is delivered and your team is working on the issues that arose from it, a tertiary event could also be described via inject, such as a building fire (from severed gas lines), trapped people (from building damage), or flooding (from severed water lines or sewer pipes).

Your job as the designer is to plot out this escalation strategy and have a clear vision of where the exercise is going so the injects match that vision.

Who develops the injects?

The exercise Design Team to the rescue! (See Chapter 3.) Your Design Team can create most or all of the exercise injects. They can write general injects, but they should really shine with injects based on their specific subject matter expertise. The format of the design team meetings is discussed in the next chapter.

Exercise inject delivery methods

There are many ways to inject information into an exercise! The only thing that may limit the choices is your imagination – and perhaps your budget.

Simplest Methods

In a Tabletop exercise, these are the two most common methods of inject delivery:

▶ *Facilitator or Controller reads injects from the inject script.* In this situation, the injects are read one-by-one and then discussed. When the issues have been thoroughly discussed, the next inject is read to the players.

▶ *Slides.* Slides allow the use of photos or other graphics, and can be more interesting for the players. The text of the inject can be displayed on the slides for all to see, along with vivid images.

Other methods

Exercise injects are inserted into Functional or Full-scale exercises using a Simulation Team, controllers, or an audio-visual tool. The following methods are most often used:

▶ Message Center forms (see Chapter 9).

▶ Phone.

▶ Walkie-talkie/Push-to-talk devices.

▶ Fax.

▶ Email.

▶ Mock broadcast, radio or video (from a local station or entity such as CNN).

▶ Mock contractor report (from your company's engineering staff or firm).

▶ Mock newspaper article (from a local newspaper).

▶ Mock website story (from news stations such as CNN or a local TV station; or from a social media site such as Facebook or Twitter).

▶ "Runner." (A person assigned to hand-deliver the inject, either on paper or by reciting the information verbally.)

▶ Actor playing a role.

Which is the best method of delivery?

The "best" delivery method will depend on your team and situation. An exercise that employs several methods of inject delivery is, of course, more interesting and varied for the players, Simulators, and controllers. Consider the following issues when selecting your delivery methods:

▶ Skill and ability.

▶ Scope and scale.

▶ Technical expertise.

▶ Budget.

Skill and ability

What is the skill, ability, and experience of team being exercised? The more capable and practiced the team, the more they will benefit from and enjoy a more sophisticated inject delivery method. A team exercising for the first time, or a team that has seen a lot of turnover may benefit from a simpler approach.

Scope and scale

What is the scope and scale of your exercise? If you have a lot of moving parts – many venues, different locations, multiple teams – you will likely need a variety of inject methods to create the story, successfully develop it, and move it along where you need it to go.

Technical expertise

If you have technical expertise available to you, then I would use it to the hilt! Many organizations have communications departments with technical teams who can develop audio and video materials. You might find some good options locally with skilled voice-over talent or local actors. Some college audio-visual departments or programs can even develop realistic materials that will excite the players and make the exercise seem like the real thing!

Budget

Of course, everything has a price. When you are developing the budget for your exercise, set aside some funds for audio-visual support, if at all possible. A professionally done radio broadcast can really set the tone for an exercise and get everyone "in the mood."

Information sources

Information will come into your exercise from a variety of sources, some that you can control, and others that you can't. It is important to recognize these multiple sources and be aware of them. One of these sources could possibly start to derail your exercise, and you need to know how to identify it, and then – if need be – "right" the exercise to keep it on track. We will discuss how to get an exercise back on track in a future chapter; for now, be aware of information that makes its way to your players from the following sources:

▶ Injects.
▶ "Making stuff up."
▶ Spontaneous information.

Injects

These are the things that you know about and can control. These, of course, are the pre-scripted injects that your Design Team has worked so hard to create. They should contain the information you want and need the players to receive.

"Making stuff up"

Exercise players have been known to start "making stuff up" as the exercise goes along. You, of course, can't control their minds, but you need to be aware that they're doing it, and what it is they're making up. Your own observations and the observations of the evaluators and controllers can help you keep an eye on this as the exercise moves along.

Spontaneous information

Simulators or the facilitator/controllers may present spontaneous information as the exercise progresses. This is likely to occur for the following reasons:

▶ *Push a particular issue.* The players might not be "getting" or understanding an important issue in the exercise. You need to interject more or different information into the exercise to push the issue.

▶ *Right a misconception.* Along the way, an assumption may have been made that needs correcting. As an example, the team may think that the power is off to a building. As it turns out, in your story, not only is the power on, but it's important that it remain on, you need to correct that misconception. This can be done by delivering an ad hoc inject to right the story.

▶ *Combat some made-up player information.* As discussed above, players will sometimes make up their own information; occasionally, their made-up information directly conflicts with your exercise design. For example, in one inject, someone asks for laptops to be delivered "right away." The Simulation Team (acting as the laptop vendor) has replied that they can't ship for at least two weeks. However, someone on the technology team declares they "magically" found all the laptops that were needed right now. Your Simulation Team (again, as the laptop vendor) will need to call back and correct that misconception: "No, we didn't ship those laptops and can't for another two weeks!"

▶ *Correct the direction the exercise is taking.* Players might have come up with an idea or assumption that is in direct conflict with your design, either due to their own agenda or because the issue wasn't clearly addressed in the design. If an assumption is being made that is going to create havoc with future injects and the story line, your Simulation Team needs to call in a spontaneous inject to correct that misconception.

Inject buckets

After doing exercises for many years, I know that injects generally revolve around five areas (or what I call "buckets"). You want to make sure that each of these "buckets" is addressed during the inject development phase of the design process:

► People.
► Facilities.
► Technology.
► Mission-critical activities.
► Communication.

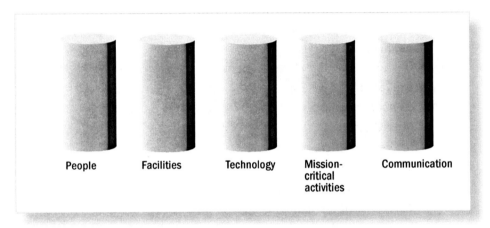

People Facilities Technology Mission-critical activities Communication

People

These injects will cover people and the things that can happen to them.

► Injects could come from:
  ▷ Employees.
  ▷ Contractors.
  ▷ The public.
  ▷ Family members.
  ▷ Ex-patriots.
  ▷ Vendors.
  ▷ Employees from other locations.
► They could be asking about:
  ▷ Injuries.
  ▷ Inability to locate someone.
  ▷ Their need for assistance.
  ▷ Their need for information ("Where do I go?" "What do I do?").
  ▷ Salary and benefits.

Facilities

▶ Facility damage as a result of the primary event, or secondary/tertiary to the primary event.

▶ Utility problems such as loss of power, gas, water, sewer, fiber optic.

▶ On-site emergency responder requests or needs.

▶ Chemical releases.

▶ Event near your facility causing issues, i.e., overturned truck, wild-land fire.

Technology

▶ Technology failures:

▷ Data center.

▷ Specific servers.

▷ Specific applications.

▷ Network (VPN, WAN).

▷ Telecommunications.

▶ Recovery issues:

▷ Bad drives.

▷ Corrupt tapes.

▷ Mis-delivered tapes.

▷ Inability to access closest hotsite for hours or days.

▶ Information security:

▶ Hacking.

▶ Denial-of-service attack.

▶ Infections (viruses, worms, etc.).

▶ Network breach.

Mission-critical activities

These injects address the mission-critical departments, functions, or processes that are now at risk as a result of this event/situation. These injects could report issues with:

▶ Vendors.

▶ Supply-chain disruption.

▶ Other key partners.

▶ Other locations.

Communication

Your communication injects should come from or be about your stakeholders:

▶ Employees.

▶ Customers, clients.

▶ Media.

▶ Investor community.

▶ Vendors.

▶ Partners.

▶ Board of directors.

▶ Government officials/Mayor/Governor/Regulators

They could be looking for:

▶ Information.

▶ Reassurance.

▶ Incident-specific information.

▶ The official company response.

Other inject topics

▶ Lifeline failures in the area:

▷ Utilities.

▷ Government action.

▷ Airports, transport, highways, local roads.

▷ Communication issues.

▶ Specific new information that moves the story forward and doesn't easily fall into any other inject "bucket."

Exercise inject sheet

Exercise injects can be organized for your exercise using a Word document table or a spreadsheet. The use of a spreadsheet can give you more options in sorting and organizing, but may limit the readability; however, either application can work well. What do you need to include when crafting an exer-

MOD 4 HW

cise inject? The key information is:

▶ Inject number.

▶ Time the inject is to be delivered.

▶ Who on the Sim Team is to deliver the inject (if applicable).

▶ Who the "caller" is supposed to be.

▶ Inject content (the "script").

Optional, but helpful, information could include:

▶ Expected actions/outcomes: A place to state the ideal result of this inject. (In a small exercise, and especially when the Design Team turns into the Simulators, I don't use this column. The Design Team cum Simulators have already discussed the "correct" answer or expected outcome during the design process.)

▶ Blank column for simulator notes.

▶ Notation indicating the method of inject transmission.

▶ Notation of which individual or team is to receive the inject.

A sample inject sheet could look like this:

Call #	Time	Sim Team Caller	Caller name, title, & dept	Call script	Notes
				RADIO BROADCAST, <<local reporter>> from <<local station>>	
			Officer <<name>>, <<city>> Police or Fire Dept.	1. Call from a public safety agency in the early stage of the exercise. 2. Call regarding traffic control: We're instituting traffic control around the building to prevent cars from entering or leaving the building and the surrounding area. No one will be allowed to leave your garage until further notice. 3. Call with follow-up about the situation: We believe now that <<update>>.	
			Media: <<local name>>, <<local paper or station>> reporter	Pick, choose, invent other calls: o We are following up on the news report about the <<issue>>. We've heard <<rumor slightly wrong>>. Is this true? o The <<paper or station>> has received reports that <<rumor slightly wrong>>. We heard reports that <<company>> takes care of its staff, but when it comes to contractors, "you're on your own." o A local station reporter, is here at the guard desk with a camera crew. They heard about the <<issue>> and that someone died, and they want to interview someone in the Command Center for a short news spot. o We're on our way over to get an interview with senior staff, ideally this would include the President, about the <<issue>>. We'll need as much information as you can give us, and we go live in 20 minutes.	

Master Scenario Events List (MSEL)

One term that you may hear in the world of exercise design is "MSEL" (often pronounced "measle"). A Master Scenario Events List (MSEL) is a chronologically sequenced outline of the simulated events or injects and key event descriptions that players will be asked to respond to during the course of the exercise. It also contains a list of expected actions resulting from the events and objectives. In other words, it is the exact same thing as the exercise inject script described above.

Key injects

In some exercises, you might want to highlight or mark injects that are tied to specific objectives or key concerns. These key injects are designed specifically to raise those issues that you want to follow during the exercise to learn how the players resolved them. An exercise will often have 4 or 5 key injects that need to be followed from inject delivery to resolution (or the end of the exercise). They should somehow be indicated on your inject sheet so you or your observers/evaluators are able to follow them. Bolded or italicized type, colored font, or a shaded row could suffice to make the key injects stand out from the others.

Key injects are identified for and followed by controllers, evaluators, and/ or the Simulation Team until they are resolved. If any key inject is not resolved adequately or properly, the Simulation Team/Controllers/Evaluators need to keep the inject "alive" until its successful resolution.

Final review

Once the injects have been fully vetted by all the team members, you still have a bit of work to do: The injects now need to be prepared for their delivery on exercise day. This entails the following:

▶ Order the injects into the sequence that they will be delivered.

▷ It's very likely that your in-process inject sheet is grouped by the persons or organizations who wrote the injects. You will need to review the topics and determine which get delivered earlier or later, which are dependent on other injects or exercise story movement, and other considerations based on the flow of the story.

▶ Determine and assign the time you want the injects to be delivered.

    ▷ Depending on how many injects you have, the experience of the team, and the complexity of the injects, this could be one inject a minute, or vary the injects to be delivered every two minutes or longer.

▶ Assign a Simulation Team member to deliver the call (if applicable).

    ▷ Select a name from the Sim Team list to place each call. You can match each caller individually to a specific inject, or you can simply rotate names through the injects.

Tips on timing injects

For the timing of the injects, I tend to "front-load" an exercise – plan the pace of calls to be a bit quicker in the beginning in order to get everyone into the game. I also try to make sure that the initial calls touch all of the teams – not just one or two – in order to engage everyone right off the bat. After the first 15 or 20 minutes, you can slow the pace down a bit (but not too much!).

As a general rule, the last inject should be delivered about 10 or 15 minutes before the scheduled end time of the exercise. Thanks to human nature, at that point – especially if they are not really engaged in the process – they can look at the clock and determine that if they simply drag their feet a little bit, it will all be over!

So here's the big tip about timing: Never deliver significant injects at the end of an exercise. It could very easily turn out to be a waste of some great injects:

▶ If they're engaged in the process, they won't have time to really work the issues.

▶ If they're not really engaged in the process (or even if they are, but are completely burned out), they could decide to "slow roll" working on them.

▶ If you have had to slow down your pace, you might not deliver all of those at the end at all.

Summary

Well-crafted and vetted exercise injects are tied to the exercise objectives and deliverables, and continue to develop the exercise story. Injects delivered using different modalities can make for a more engaging and interesting experience. Thoughtful and well-designed exercise injects will help you reach your exercise objectives.

CHAPTER 7

Where the magic is created – design team

Design team meetings

Before the Design Team meetings can begin, it is best to have an exercise plan and narrative that are very close to being complete. In other words, you can have some outstanding questions on minor things like EOC location and exact timing of the team breaks, but the bulk of your exercise structure and story line must be done in order for the Design Team to "sink their teeth" into their work.

In my experience, most Design Team meetings last between 90 minutes and two hours. They work equally well when held face-to-face or as a virtual meeting (conference call). I routinely hold Design Team meetings by conference call, and find them to be a highly efficient and effective use of everyone's time.

How many meetings should you have?

How many meetings you need really depends on the length of the exercise, the complexity of the exercise, and how many exercises you are designing. For a half-day or four-hour exercise, you can probably get by with three meetings. For two-part exercises, or if you are having an all-day (6-hour) exercise, it's more likely you will need more meetings, probably four or five (see chart).

Design team meetings are usually held every other week. You don't want to lose the team's momentum by waiting too long between meetings; con-

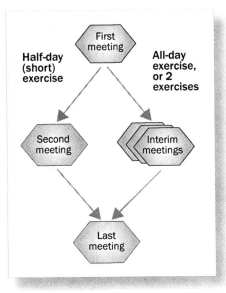

versely, the team needs time to do their homework (writing injects or doing their 'trench coat research').

Most of the all-day exercises that we conduct are comprised of two parts, both focused more on business continuity. The first part of the exercise usually starts after the life safety issues have started to wind down. For the second part, we normally "advance the clock" two or three days after the initial event in order to push the team to really address continuity issues and the impact of a sustained operation.

"Typical" design team meeting structure – half-day (short) exercise

First meeting

The first meeting is your opportunity to set expectations and lay down the foundation for success. You will have a lot to cover in this meeting. A sample agenda could include the following topics:

- ▶ Orientation to exercises and exercise design:
  - ▷ Ascertain who has been in an exercise before.
  - ▷ Review the type of exercise you are conducting.
  - ▷ Review the team positions that will be exercised. If possible, review the names of the team member who will be fulfilling each spot.
  - ▷ Discuss the expectations and role of the Design Team.
- ▶ Review the Design Team meeting schedule. (These should have been put on the Design Team members' calendars already.)
- ▶ Review the exercise plan, especially the exercise objectives.
- ▶ Review the narrative. Validate that the Design Team agrees it is a viable scenario.
- ▶ Review the concept of an exercise inject, and begin brainstorming ideas for injects.
- ▶ Issue the first homework assignment (see next section) **AND** assign a due date for the homework. (This is very important; a task with no due date often doesn't get done.) See "What happens between Design Team meetings?" section below for advice on scheduling homework

due dates.

▶ Reaffirm the next Design Team meeting date.

Second meeting

The goal of the second meeting is to finalize the exercise plan, including the narrative, and review the homework assignment.

▶ Review the exercise plan:

▷ Review any changes that you made to the exercise plan (based on the team's feedback or other contributions from the first meeting).

▷ Review the narrative. Ideally, you will want the narrative to be finalized at the end of this meeting. If the storyline remains in flux, shifting and changing, it can impact the exercise injects. If it is tinkered with continuously, it becomes increasingly difficult to make sure the story is straight and put together seamlessly.

▶ Review all of the homework.

▷ Review each inject one by one. In addition to verifying that each inject makes sense individually, you also need to make sure they make sense collectively. Remember, this is like writing a book, a movie, or a screenplay – the story needs to flow like one head has written it, not a multi-headed person!

▷ Validate the information and the details of each inject.

▷ Make sure the proposed caller isn't participating as a player in the exercise. (Someone who is on a team would not be calling in to the EOC with an issue.)

▷ Verify you have enough injects for the length of exercise you are designing. (A good rule of thumb is 20 to 25 injects per hour, but this will depend on the maturity of the team – fewer injects for a "green" team, more for a more experienced team. In the long run, it's better to have too many injects and cut the ones you don't need than to have too few and have to "wing it" on exercise day if you run out of injects before you reach the end of the exercise.)

▷ After you have reviewed the last inject, ask the Design Team,

"What are we missing?" Your goal is to uncover any glaring gaps, especially in any of the five core areas. You want to make sure you have adequately addressed:

> People – life safety concerns.
> Facilities issues.
> Technology.
> Communication.
> Mission-critical activities that are at risk.

NOTE: Put yourself in the shoes of the people going through this situation. What would you be thinking and feeling if you were in these circumstances? Have the injects touched on those issues?

▶ Step back and assess where you are. There will usually be a need to assign a second round of homework to the team. Very often you will need to develop more injects to cover specific areas that were missed, or the team may need to revise existing injects that didn't quite hit the mark.

▷ If necessary, assign this second homework assignment. Don't forget to assign the next due date. (See "What happens between Design Team meetings?" section below for advice on scheduling homework due dates.)

▶ Reaffirm next Design Team meeting date.

Last meeting

▶ Do a *light* review of the exercise plan and narrative to ensure no new information has surfaced since the last meeting that would have an impact on your planning.

▶ Review all of the homework.

▷ Review each inject one-by-one as you did in the last meeting, asking the same questions and addressing the same concerns.

▶ Once again, after you have reviewed the last inject, ask "What are we missing?" Make sure you have covered the five core areas.

At this point, stand back and consider where you are in the process. Do you feel like you are done? Does everyone seem on board? Does it seem like there are a lot of loose ends?

▶ If you believe you're on track, and if the meeting time permits, the end of this meeting is a good opportunity to discuss the exercise day with the Design Team, to give them a brief glimpse of what to expect (see Chapter 11).

▶ If you believe you are not done, for whatever reason, you will need to determine if you can resolve the issues via phone calls and/or emails, or if you need to schedule another meeting before exercise day. You may simply need some additional research, or you may need a significant number of new injects developed or completely redesigned. Assign the appropriate homework and due date, and, if necessary, get the final meeting date and time on team members' calendars.

▶ If the Design Team will be acting as the Simulation Team on the exercise day, confirm when the Simulation Team training will be held, as well as the exercise date.

"Typical" Design Team meeting structure – full-day exercise

First meeting

This meeting will be structured basically the same way as a short exercise.

The first meeting is your opportunity to set expectations and lay down the foundation for success. You will have a lot to cover in this meeting. A sample agenda could include the following topics:

▶ Orientation to exercises and exercise design:
  ▷ Ascertain who has been in an exercise before.
  ▷ Review the type of exercise you are performing.
  ▷ Review the team positions that will be exercised. If possible, review the names of the team member who will be fulfilling each spot.
  ▷ Discuss the expectations and role of the Design Team.

▶ Review the Design Team meeting schedule. (These should have been put on the Design Team members' calendars already.)

▶ Review the exercise plan, especially the exercise objectives.

▶ Review the exercise narrative. Validate that the Design Team agrees it is a viable scenario.

▷ If you are doing a two-part exercise, review the narrative for exercise part one.

▷ If you are doing one, longer exercise, review the entire narrative.

▶ Review the concept of an exercise inject, and begin brainstorming ideas for injects.

▶ Issue the first homework assignment (see next section) **AND** assign a due date for the homework. (This is very important; a task with no due date often doesn't get done.) See "What happens between Design Team meetings?" section below for advice on scheduling homework due dates.

▶ Reaffirm the next Design Team meeting date.

Second meeting

The goal of the second meetings for a longer exercise or two-part exercises is very similar to the second meeting for a shorter exercise.

▶ Review the exercise plan:

▷ Review any changes that you made to the exercise plan (based on the team's feedback or other contributions from the first meeting).

▷ Review the narrative.

> If you are doing a two-part exercises, ideally, you will want the narrative for exercise part one to be finalized at the end of this meeting. If the storyline remains in flux, shifting and changing, it can impact the exercise injects. If it is tinkered with continuously, it becomes increasingly difficult to make sure the story is straight and put together seamlessly.

> If you are doing a longer exercise, you will want to have the fundamental structure of the exercise in place and agreed to. Again, if the story is not pinned down, it affects the schedule for writing and reviewing injects, and can make your story seem "choppy."

▶ Review all of the homework.

▷ Review each inject one by one. In addition to verifying that each inject makes sense individually, you also need to make sure they make sense collectively. Remember, this is like writing a book, a movie, or a screenplay – the story needs to flow like one head has written it, not a multi-headed person!

▷ Validate the information and the details of each inject.

▷ Make sure the proposed caller isn't participating as a player in the exercise. (Someone who is on a team would not be calling in to the EOC with an issue.)

▷ Verify you have enough injects for the length of exercise you are designing. (A good rule of thumb is 20 to 25 injects per hour, but this will depend on the maturity of the team – fewer injects for a "green" team, more for a more experienced team. In the long run, it's better to have too many injects and cut the ones you don't need, than to have too few and have to "wing it" on exercise day if you run out of injects before you reach the end of the exercise.)

▷ After you have reviewed the last inject, ask the Design Team, "What are we missing?" Your goal is to uncover any glaring gaps, especially in any of the five core areas. You want to make sure you have adequately addressed:

> People – life safety concerns.

> Facilities issues.

> Technology.

> Communication.

> Mission-critical activities that are at risk.

NOTE: Put yourself in the shoes of the people going through this situation. What would you be thinking and feeling if you were in these circumstances? Have the injects touched on those issues?

At this point, stand back and consider where you are in the process. Very often, you will need to develop more injects to cover specific areas that were missed, or the team may need to revise existing injects that didn't quite hit the mark.

▶ If you feel like you are done with exercise one, review the scenario for exercise two, and brainstorm possible injects.

▶ If you feel like you're not done with exercise one, assign more homework for exercise one (more injects, more research).

▶ Review the appropriate homework assignment and due date. (See "What happens between Design Team meetings?" section below for advice on scheduling homework due dates.)

▶ Affirm the next meeting date.

Third meeting

The goal of the third meeting (and any other meetings you may hold between the second meeting and the last meeting) are repeats of the second meeting: to address outstanding issues from the previous meeting. Move the team's attention to the second narrative as appropriate.

Last meeting

▶ Do a light review of the exercise plan and narrative to ensure no new information has surfaced since the last meeting that would have an impact on your planning.

▶ Review all of the homework.

▷ Review each inject one-by-one as you did in the last meeting, asking the same questions and addressing the same concerns.

▶ Once again, after you have reviewed the last inject, ask "What are we missing?" Make sure you have covered the five core areas.

At this point, stand back and consider where you are in the process. Do you feel like you are done? Does everyone seem on board? Does it seem like there are a lot of loose ends?

▶ If you believe you're on track, and if the meeting time permits, this is a good opportunity to discuss the exercise day with the Design Team, to give them a brief glimpse of what to expect (see Chapter 11).

▶ If you believe you are not done, for whatever reason, you will need to determine if you can resolve the issues via phone calls and/or emails, or if you need to schedule another meeting before exercise day. You may simply need some additional research, or you may need a significant number of new injects developed or completely redesigned. Assign the appropriate homework and due date, and, if necessary, get the final meeting date and time on team members' calendars.

▶ If the Design Team will be acting as the Simulation Team on the exercise day, confirm when the Simulation Team training will be held, as well as the exercise date.

What happens between Design Team meetings?

Between the scheduled meetings, you (as the designer) will be on the lookout for questions or issues that arise as a result of the meetings. You will also be consolidating the injects that come in from the Design Team members.

It is a good practice to schedule the homework's due date to be a few days before the next meeting. This will allows you time to review the injects, do any "clean up" that might be necessary (spelling, punctuation, grammar), or flag potential issues or inconsistencies that may appear (missing caller names, one inject directly conflicting with another inject written by someone else). The more you can do before the next meeting, the more productive the actual meeting will be for the entire team.

Look for injects that might need a bit of work:

▶ The inject isn't clear. After reading it, you just aren't sure what the writer was trying to get at.

▶ The inject has incomplete information. For example, the caller name is missing, a key business process isn't named.

▶ The inject doesn't require the player to have to decide, validate, consider, or defer, or the inject doesn't provide new information. As you remember from Chapter 6, injects should do one of those five things. If it's not, then what is it doing?

To speed up the Design Team meeting itself, if time permits before the next meeting, you may find it helpful to send back specific questions to the Design Team members. Ask them to clarify your issues and questions, and to respond back to you before the next meeting.

You may also find that some people "get" the concept of inject writing right away and can write good injects all day long. Others may need a bit of coaching, which you can provide between meetings. That one-on-one coaching can sometimes make a huge difference in the quality of injects you receive, and consequently make the meetings themselves far more productive.

Once the injects have been cleaned up and massaged to your satisfaction, send out a revised set of injects prior to the next meeting, along with a list of outstanding issues and questions to help facilitate a timely meeting. An issues page can consolidate questions, outline items that are missing, or indicate the need for names and titles in one place.

Exercise Design Team meeting checklist

Use this checklist as a guide in setting up your Design Team meetings.

Prior to the first meeting

▶ Select your Design Team members.

▶ Develop a list of meeting dates.

▶ Secure a conference bridge or conference room for the meetings.

▶ Issue meeting invitations. Follow up with any team member who declines the meeting.

▶ Finalize the draft exercise plan and narrative.

First meeting

▶ Give an orientation to exercises and exercise design:

▷ Ascertain who has been in an exercise before.

▷ Review the type of exercise you are performing.

▷ Review the team positions that will be exercised. If possible, review the names of the team member who will be fulfilling each spot.

▷ Discuss the expectations and role of the Design Team.

▶ Review the Design Team meeting schedule. (These should have been put on the Design Team members' calendars already.)

▶ Review the exercise plan, especially the exercise objectives.

▶ Review the narrative. Validate that the Design Team agrees it is a viable scenario.

▶ Review the concept of an exercise inject.

▷ Begin brainstorming ideas for injects.

▷ Issue the first homework assignment.

▷ Assign a due date for the homework.

▶ Issue the first homework assignment (see next section) **AND** assign a due date for the homework. (This is very important; a task with no due date often doesn't get done.) See "What happens between Design Team meetings?" section above for advice on scheduling homework due dates.

▶ Reaffirm the next Design Team meeting date.

In between meetings

▶ Follow-up with team members as necessary (questions you might have, homework not received).

Subsequent meetings

▶ Review the exercise plan:
  ▷ Review any changes that you made to the exercise plan.
  ▷ Review the narrative.

▶ Review all of the homework.
  ▷ Review each inject one by one.
  ▷ Validate the information and the details of each inject.
  ▷ Make sure the proposed caller isn't participating as a player in the exercise.
  ▷ Verify you have enough injects for the length of exercise you are designing.

▶ Ask the question, "What are we missing?" Make sure you have adequately addressed:
  ▷ People – life safety concerns.
  ▷ Facilities issues.
  ▷ Technology.
  ▷ Communication.
  ▷ Mission-critical activities that are at risk.

▶ Stand back and review where you are.
  ▷ Assign homework as appropriate.
  ▷ Assign due date for homework.

▶ Affirm next meeting date.

▷ If last meeting:
> Discuss the exercise day with the Design Team.
> If there are still outstanding issues, determine if you need to schedule another meeting to resolve them. If so, schedule the meeting.
> If the Design Team will be acting as the Simulation Team on the exercise day, confirm date and time of the Simulation Team training and the exercise.

Summary

Your job as the exercise facilitator is to "hold the vision" of the exercise. Crisp Design Team agendas, good facilitation skills and a clear roadmap are the things that make Design Team meetings successful and fulfill the vision of the exercise.

CHAPTER 8

Make your exercise sizzle – audio-visual tools

A picture is worth a thousand words.[7]

Whenever we design an exercise, we want our participants to get into their role and feel as though this incident was really happening. One effective way to do this is to use audio-visual tools or training aids. Using these tools or aids effectively can help reinforce your verbal message significantly, while stimulating the brains of your exercise players, and tapping into different learning modalities.

I hear, I forget.
I see, I remember.
I do, I understand.
— Confucius [8]

By creating and using effective supporting material, you have a higher likelihood of holding exercise players' interest while helping them gain, retain, recognize, recall, and later use the information to which they are exposed. A caveat, though, as you design your audio-visual materials: don't forget that their intended purpose is to reinforce your primary message. Sometimes that basic premise can get lost in the excitement of designing fun and engaging materials.

Using audio-visual tools to progress the story

Before you start planning which audio-visual tools you will use, you need to plot out the exercise story development, starting with the baseline narra-

---

7   A quote attributed to several different nationalities and entities. http://www.phrases.org.uk/
    meanings/a-picture-is-worth-a-thousand-words.html
8   Confucius http://www.quotationspage.com/quote/25848.html

tive, and working through the exercise inject script. This concept is similar to filmmakers using storyboards to develop the plot of a movie. The idea is to map out the progression of the story in sequence, using pictures, images, and/ or words. Once you understand the flow and progression of your story, you can determine what exercise injects would be appropriate to introduce via an audio-visual tool.

The four most common audio-visual tools for enhancing the exercise experience are:

▶ Slides with images.
▶ Radio broadcasts.
▶ Videos.
▶ Mock documents.

Slides with images

A low-cost, but still effective, tool is the use of images in a slide presentation, such as PowerPoint. This would be most commonly used for Orientation or Tabletop exercises to deliver the initial narrative and then to introduce any subsequent injects or information. Images can be highly effective in mentally taking the players to where you want them to be.

Where do you find the images? Lots of places!

▶ *Take your own pictures.* I always have a camera with me and will take shots of anything that looks like it might be useful at a later date. Look with "new eyes" at fire trucks, police scenes, fires, industrial sites, accidents, ambulances, or any other responders you may encounter.

▶ *Check internally.* If you have an internal Communications Department, they may have stock footage of previous incidents that you could use as well.

▶ *Check with official organizations.* Your state or local Office of Emergency Services, Fire and Police departments will likely have stock photos in their image files.

▶ *Search likely websites.* You can use images from many websites as long as you give them credit in your work. Be sure to check with the website first, though!

▶ *Research stock photos.* Stock photo houses with a wide array of images abound on the Internet. Most charge a fee to use the image; some allow limited free downloads.

▶ *Research trade associations.* Some professional trade associations may have appropriate images for use. Again, some may charge a fee, some may allow usage with a citation. Check first!

When building a presentation with powerful images, use just enough text to tell the story but not to distract from the image. Keep the slides to a handful. You need enough to tell the story, but not so many that you numb them to sleep with a PowerPoint lecture.

Radio broadcast

The radio broadcast is a powerful tool and can be used to set the stage at the beginning of the exercise. A mid-exercise broadcast can also be used to drop in new information as a "breaking news story" during the exercise.

Starting the exercise with a broadcast can really set the tone and put the players into the mindset that this has really happened. The initial broadcast usually reiterates the basic information that's contained in the exercise plan narrative. This can be helpful as the players are just starting to "wrap their brain" around the incident. Hearing the story again via a broadcast can be helpful.

If you have some major twists in the middle of the exercise, consider using a broadcast to introduce those as "breaking news" stories. These should be short broadcasts, between 90 seconds and two minutes. The goal is to drop this new information into the mix and get out, like a "reporter" who quickly updates the situation and then says "back to the studio." This can heighten the energy level of the players, get participants' blood pumping again, and reinvigorate the situation.

Begin by determining which radio station will be "broadcasting" the story. Would this incident have national implications? In that case, it may be from a national news station. Is it a more local event? Then it would more likely be covered by your local radio new stations. Pick an appropriate station and listen to them to get a sense of their style, what they are like, and how their broadcasters sound.

Plan your broadcast to be between three and four minutes; no longer than four minutes. People's attention will drift away if you go too much longer than that. If you plan to do the broadcast yourself, write the script, then practice it saying it aloud several times before recording. This practice will serve you well when it comes time to turn the microphone to "on." A story that reads well on paper may sound awkward and stilted when spoken.

Practice and modify, paying close attention to how the words flow, where the punctuation indicates a rest, and how long the sentences are. A good rule is that between 125 and 150 words equals one minute of speaking – depending on how fast you talk, of course – but be careful to pace yourself. In general, most people speak faster than a normal broadcast, so listen to your recording and determine if it sounds rushed. Re-record it until it flows evenly and at a good pace. Don't forget the volume of your voice, too. Don't shout, but remember to project your voice.

We are lucky enough to have access to a fabulous Bay Area voice-over talent with his own studio to produce our broadcasts. He records them, adds appropriate sound effects, mixes them, and then sends them to our office via email as an MP3 file. You may be able to find a similar resource at a local college from their broadcasting program or the campus radio station.

Video

Video production is highly effective but more expensive. If a picture is worth a thousand words, then moving pictures must be worth a few million. An opening video can be an even more powerful way to kick off your exercise.

Create the script for the video in the same way as you would a radio broadcast. If you are acquiring video images from a variety of sources, check that the image quality is the same. Mixing professional video stock footage with video pulled from YouTube can work, but you may need to spend a lot of time to make it meld together seamlessly. There are many stock video companies on the Internet to choose from, and many companies who can do the work for you. Be aware, however, that it could get costly.

Mock documents

What kinds of documents could help move your story along? What about a newspaper story "pulled from the web"? Maybe a posting on a consumer website? How about a blogger who posts something following your incident? A 'tweet' that goes viral? What if you need your building contractor to issue a "building report" on the damage sustained as a result of your event? Those are all examples of what we call "mock documents."

To get started, pick an entity that would likely follow your incident, "dummy up" a document to make it look like it came from them, and then use it as an inject. However, be sure that anyone who may find the paper knows it's not real. Place in large, bold letters at the top of every page, "THIS IS AN EXERCISE DOCUMENT" to avoid having a War of the Worlds effect.

Mock newspaper article

Before you write an article, spend some time online and look at the sites you are trying to emulate. Go to national sites like The New York Times, Chicago Tribune, or Los Angeles Times, as well as your local paper's site. Notice the layout, the format and the writing style. Pay attention to headlines, bylines, and the images they use.

Do a search on that site and see if your organization has been written about before. This can be a helpful tool, and make your current story even more real to the players. Imagine reading about your current incident and then the "writer" talks about the previous event, just like a "real" story would. Bringing up older stories really pushes the Communications team to develop a comprehensive response, not only addressing the new issues, but also thinking about how to handle those old references as well. It is also helpful to print their articles to see how they look in the print format.

Mock website coverage

What other sites might report on your incident? Think about social media sites, such as Facebook or Twitter. What about consumer or watchdog sites, or blogs like the Huffington Post or the Nation? You might even consider a mock Wikipedia page, as they often post stories within minutes or a few hours of a major incident. If you aren't sure who might follow your organization, speak to your Communications department – they will know.

Mock contractor report

If you need your exercise players to learn about some building damage from your scenario's fire or flood, you can choose to have someone inject the information ("I just walked by and saw a big hole where the first floor loading platform used to be!"). Or you could write a "report" from someone chartered to investigate the damage.

Your organization likely has a building contractor, structural engineer, or maintenance staff either on staff or a separate firm on retainer. Find out the appropriate entity who would be reporting the information, and provide the "report" at a specified time during the exercise. Sample information could be items such as:

▶ "After a more thorough inspection of the buildings, we found that the original mold source was in the gym on the 5th floor of the A building, apparently starting when one of the pipes into the men's shower area burst sometime in mid-May. A second leak has gone unnoticed for at least 3 weeks, with water slowly being absorbed into all porous items as it spread."

▶ "Numerous bullet holes in reception desk, waiting area furniture, and walls. Glass double-doors completely shattered, security access mechanism irreparable. Extensive bloodstains on carpet, on wall next to desk, and on wall adjacent to elevators."

▶ "Roof damage to 35% of the roof at the southern end of the building. Water has penetrated into the South elevator and mechanical penthouses. The penthouse façade has been badly damaged on the south and west sides. 90% of exterior tempered glass screen elements have been ripped off building and are lying shattered in the street and on the 6th floor terrace."

As with other mock items, be sure to indicate "THIS IS AN EXERCISE DOCUMENT" prominently on the report.

Summary

The goal of an audio-visual inject is to inject a feeling of realism. A well-crafted audio-visual tool will help instill a sense of reality to your exercise, as well as move the story line along. Carefully think through the entire exercise inject script and determine where an audio-visual injection could really give your exercise some spark!

Supporting documents to make it all work – additional background exercise documents

By now, you know you need an exercise plan and exercise injects to make an exercise work. What else do you need? In general, there are several more documents that should be considered as necessary for every exercise, and a few more that are optional, depending on the type and the complexity of the exercise.

Necessary documents:

▶ Participant evaluation.

▶ Document summary.

▶ Evaluator/Controller/Observer form.

Optional documents:

▶ Phone directory.

▶ Executive briefing.

▶ Message Center form.

▶ Simulation Team evaluation.

Necessary documents

Participant evaluation

The participant evaluation form is an important part of the evaluation process. If you follow the recommendations of this book, you will hold a verbal debrief at the conclusion of the exercise, where you will likely get a lot of constructive information. However, it is also important to seek the player's feedback in writing as well – not everyone will bring up a topic in public, but they are often more willing to express something anonymously in writing, especially if it's a politically charged topic. We always include a summary of the results of these evaluations in our After-Action Report (see Chapter 15).

The evaluation can be used to seek an overall reaction to the participant's exercise experience, as well as provide specific feedback about key issues you are interested in learning more about. It is helpful to have two types of response questions to meet the feedback needs of the players. Design about half of the questions as ranked answers (such as a range from "strongly agree" to "strongly disagree" or from "met expectations" to "did not meet expectations"). The remainder of the questions should allow for short, written responses. Areas to consider include:

▶ Perceived value of the exercise.

▶ Adequacy of the existing plan(s).

▶ The exercise itself – what worked, what needs improvement.

▶ Future training and exercise needs.

▶ Suggestions for improvement.

A word of caution, however – keep an eye on the number of questions you ask. Too few questions and the participants may form an opinion that you don't really want their impressions. However, too many questions and you may find that they get overwhelmed and stop answering anything – you'll find yourself with a lot of responses to the first few questions and a lot of blanks for the last few.

The following is a sample of participant evaluation questions.

PARTICIPANT EVALUATION QUESTIONS SAMPLE

Please circle one

	Strongly Disagree		Neutral		Strongly Agree
1. The exercise design was realistic.	1	2	3	4	5
2. The scenario was a 'real-world' (likely) event.	1	2	3	4	5
3. The exercise encouraged 'hands-on' participation.	1	2	3	4	5
4. The facilitator was effective.	1	2	3	4	5
5. The exercise met my expectations.	1	2	3	4	5
6. I have a clear understanding of how my team would response in an incident.	1	2	3	4	5

7. Overall, what did you think of the exercise?

8. What did you think was the most helpful?

9. What could we improve on?

10. What are the three top things that you think your team needs to do to be prepared for the most likely incident expected to cause a business interruption?

"Paper or Plastic?"

Unfortunately, in the paper-versus-plastic (or digital, in this case) decision, my experience is that it is best to use an old-fashioned piece of paper and distribute it at the conclusion of the exercise, rather than using an electronic survey tool. With web-based surveys (such as Survey Monkey, Zoomerang, or Surveygizmo), I have found that the return rate is quite poor in comparison to a paper form handed out right after the exercise concludes. While most people have good intentions of completing a survey after they get back to their "real life," they seem to find that their "real life" gets in the way, and the survey never gets completed, whether it's paper or digital.

Document summary

How do you keep all of these documents organized? What documents do you need and when? Who gets what, and in what format? There can be a lot of documentation to keep track of. A document summary form can help keep you on-target in the exercise design process, as well as provide guidance for exercise day document production.

The document summary notes the following:

▶ Each document required for the exercise. Include anything that any of the players would receive. This would not only include the players, but the Simulation Team, control team, and others.

▶ Each audio-visual inject and any AV requirements (e.g., radio and video broadcasts may need an MP4 or DVD player).

▶ Printing instructions for documents. How many copies should be printed? Will they be black and white or in color? Should they be on special paper?

▶ The recipient. Who receives what document? For example, the injects would normally be handed out to the Simulation Team, not all the players; however, the participant evaluation should go to everyone.

A sample document summary sheet is shown below:

SAMPLE DOCUMENT SUMMARY SHEET

Scenario: Hurricane

To Do List – Documents Needed

Items needed	Printing instructions	Status	Who receives it
Exercise plan 1	B/W	Done V1R10_20100218	Everyone
Broadcast 1	n/a	Done	n/a
Exercise plan 2	B/W	Done V1R9_20100218	Everyone
Inputs 2	B/W	Sequenced & timed V1R11_20100218	Sim Team/Evaluators/Facilitator
MC Forms completed	Color	Done MC_V1R11_20100220	One copy – Facilitator to hand out
Broadcast 2	n/a	Done	n/a
News article (Herald)	Color copies	Done V1R1_20100213	Everyone
Exercise plan 3	B/W	Done V1R11_20100218	Everyone
Inputs 3	B/W	Sequenced & timed V1R6_20100218	Sim Team/Evaluators/RP
MC Forms completed	Color	Done MC_V1R6_20100218	One copy – RP to hand out
Executive briefing (three exercises)	Send as a pdf to executives	Done V1R6_20100218	Send to executives in an email
Phone directory	Color paper please	Done v1r2_20100218	Everyone
Participant evaluation	B/W	Done V1R2_20100209	Everyone
Sim Team evaluation	B/W	Done V1R1_20100209	Sim Team
Evaluator form	B/W	Done V1R1_20100208	Evaluators only (4)

Observer forms (for evaluators, controllers, and general observers)

Having an observer (or observers) provide feedback to you can be immensely helpful, allowing you to have "eyes" into more corners of the action. Whether their role is as evaluator, controller, or observer, giving them an organized place to capture their observations gives you a leg up on getting back their thoughts. The basic observer form should include:

▶ A reiteration of the evaluators'/controllers'/observers' role that day.

▶ A few pointers on how to do that role.

▶ A restatement of the exercise objectives. (This provides a handy reminder as they go about their work, as well as emphasizing the importance of those objectives.)

▶ Space for the writer to make notes. Rather than giving them a large, free-form space, we provide sheets with two columns labeled "What worked well?" and "What needs improvement?" This focuses their observations, usually channeling them to concrete thoughts about what they've observed.

This form is the beneficiary of all of the Evaluator/Controller/Observer notes. If they will be hand-writing their notes, everyone should be asked to write with "the best handwriting you can muster." If they prefer, they could type up their comments and send back to the facilitator via email as soon as possible. The key thing is that you want their observations, comments, and findings back, so make it as easy for them as possible! (As with the paper evaluation forms, we prefer the immediacy of paper forms which can be collected at the end of the exercise.)

A sample observer sheet is shown on the next page.

Optional documents

Phone directory

Phone directories are used in functional and full-scale exercises. The phone directory is a tool used to close the communication gap and allows you, the designer, to control the environment.

The directory contains the phone numbers, fax numbers, and/or email addresses of those "outside" entities that exercise participants are likely to call. All of these numbers, of course, dial to the Simulators. (The only calls to the real outside world should be those that you approve, otherwise you risk losing control of the story.) The directory should also include a number of "generic" entities. In our exercises, we refer to them as "Genius of-all-trades" or "Jack-" or "Jill-of-all-trades." Since you probably can't think of everyone that the players may need to call, these roles represent anyone that is not already listed in the directory. It's one more tool allowing you control over the exercise environment.

SAMPLE OBSERVER SHEET

Evaluator Name   **Team Assignment**

Exercise Evaluator Form

Role of the Evaluator

The exercise design team has developed these objectives with a series of metrics for the exercise. The evaluators are to use the metrics to determine if the objectives have been met. We understand that this will be somewhat subjective by the evaluator and you can't be everywhere at once, just do the best you can. The following methods may be used:

- Observe participants.
- Look at situation boards and reporting forms.
- Look at any reports.
- Talk with participants.
- Be a "fly on the wall" to listen into conversations and informal briefings.

Exercise Objectives by Team

1. <<list objectives here>>

Exercise Metrics

The above objectives will be evaluated on feedback using three methodologies: the debrief sessions, written evaluations, and observations by the evaluator and facilitator in the exercise environment.

Please return your written comments to exercise facilitator at the end of the day.

Jobs Well Done	Areas for Improvement

Providing a phone directory and having a live Simulation Team member respond back to all injects and playing the outside world, the exercise players really have to solve the problems. They are less likely to get away with just "snapping their fingers" and have the issue magically go away. This really helps hold players' feet to the fire, makes them accountable, and allows them to deepen their own skills, mature their plans, and strengthen the program.

Phone and phone directory tips

▶ Use landlines whenever possible. It's true that in today's 'connected' world you could use cell phones – but remember that batteries die, reception can be shaky, and lost calls happen on even the most "on" network. With a landline, you avoid those problems, and have the added benefit of allowing the call to roll to voicemail if the person is on the line.

▶ Have a fax machine number for the Sim Team. Players may be asked to provide information or reports; have them fax it to the Sim Team. The machine doesn't need to be in the same room with the Sim Team, but it should be close by.

▶ Print the directory on a brightly colored paper. During an exercise, paper accumulates. Having the directory on neon-colored paper makes it easier to find in the sea of white paper!

▶ Consider having the following tools to simulate communications:

▷ Dummy email address for all simulation communications to the Sim Team.

▷ Dummy company hotline number. This allows the Communication team an opportunity to actually post a message, practicing elements such as length, tone, and volume. This allows everyone in the room to listen to an authentic message crafted just for the occasion, without worrying that someone outside the exercise might call the real number and hear about "the fire that affected the main campus." Having a dummy number also eliminates concerns about forgetting to change the real hotline message back to your default "there is no emergency to report" message. (Think that doesn't happen? Think again – I have checked those "real" emergency numbers a few weeks after some of my exercises and have found that the exercise message is still up. Yikes!)

A sample phone directory is shown below:

ABC Bank Exercise Phone Directory

Exercise Simulation Team – They create the world for you!

When calling the Simulation Team, please remember three things:
1. *Remember the Genius-of-all-trades can be anyone you want them to be!*
2. *When calling the Sim Team they will answer the phone with "May I help you?"*
   * *Tell them who you are looking for! They are the OUTSIDE WORLD.*
3. *If you need to find out "real information" (a fact) from a ABC Bank partner or department, you may call them directly – tell them you are in an exercise (without the details) and need information to answer a question or resolve a problem.*

Simulation Team	Phone	Simulation Team	Phone
ABC Bank: Any executive	8113	Department	
ABC Bank: Any foreign office (UK, Asia)	8111	Miami-Dade Transit (MDT)	8112
		National Hurricane Center	8114
ABC Bank: Incident Mgmt Team (HQ)	9800	National Oceanic and Atmospheric Administration (NOAA)	8111
Contract Security	8112		
Contractors, any	8114	Office supply vendor	8112
Dept of Homeland Security	8112	Phone service – Cell, any vendor	8114
Family Assistance Program	8114		
FBI	8111	Police Department, any	8111
Financial Institution, any	8113	Regulators, any	8113
Fire Department, any	8112	Security guard company	8112
Florida Power and Light	8114	Shipping vendors such as Fed Ex, USPS	8114
Genius-of-all-trades	8112		
Genius-of-all-trades	8114	Software companies or products, any	8111
Genius-of-all-trades	8111		
Genius-of-all-trades	8113	Technology vendors, hardware, any	8113
Hospital, any	8112		
Hotels, any	8114	Telecommunications hardware vendor, any	8112
Insurance, any	8111		
Market Conditions	8113	Telephone: Local carrier	8114
Media, any electronic	8112	Telephone: Long distance, MCI, ATT, Sprint	8111
Media, any print	8114		
Miami-Dade County, Department of Emergency Management & Homeland Security	8111	Transportation vendors, i.e. buses, shuttles, cabs	8113
		Weather forecast	8113
Miami-Dade County, Water	8113		

Executive briefing

Executive briefings most commonly are found when doing Functional and Full-scale exercises. They are a great training tool for several reasons:

▶ It allows everyone (both executives and the exercise players) to learn his or her role at the time of an incident.

▶ As with the players themselves, this practice helps instill behaviors in the executives that can be recalled as "muscle memory" at the time of an incident.

▶ It gives the executives a real understanding of your program, the work that goes into the planning process, and the strength of your team. The more the team is practiced in what it does and demonstrates that to the executive during a briefing, the more it allows the executive to assume his or her more "executive-like" roles when an incident occurs. It can provide them reassurance that the tactical duties will be well managed, leaving them to the strategic role they should assume.

The executive briefing document prepares the executives to assume their role in an exercise. It tells them everything they need to know in advance, so they can attend the briefing prepared and ready to ask those "executive-like" questions. The document should contain the following information:

▶ An outline of their specific role expectations. They will want to know exactly what is to be expected of them.

▶ An option of how they can participate. If they will be calling in, it should contain the dial-in number (and passcode as appropriate); if they will be attending in person, it should direct them to the appropriate place. Don't forget to tell them what time to attend!

▶ An outline of necessary background information regarding the exercise, including the artificialities, assumptions, and the full narrative.

▶ Optional: A list of "executive issues" they might want to focus on. Think of this as a "Cliffs Notes" section in case they didn't read the document completely.

The briefing document can be sent to them one or two days before the exercise, or it can be provided to them on the day of the exercise. (If you give it out in advance of the actual exercise, don't forget to include instructions about not sharing the narrative with anyone. After all, your Design Team has been so good about keeping the storyline under wraps, you don't want the plot to escape from the executives!)

Some sample executive briefing instructions are shown below:

▶ "When you call into the Executive Emergency conference bridge line, the Incident Commander will greet you and conduct an update briefing with your team."

▶ "Your task is to play your 'usual executive role' by asking pertinent questions on how this situation is impacting employees, regions, and the ability of team to continue to operate the business."

▶ "We ask that you stay in role, play this situation as if it is really happening. You are there to receive a briefing on the current status of this significant and on-going event."

▶ "If this were a real event, since this is an on-going event, this would not be your first briefing. In a real event you would, of course, have had several briefings prior to this call."

Some sample executive briefing key issues are shown below:

▶ "Care of missing, dead, or injured employees."

▶ "Inability to continue processing mission-critical applications for 4 days."

▶ "Inability to occupy main campus building for up to 3 months."

▶ "Effect of incident on company stock price."

Message center forms

There are some instances in which you will deliver injects to the players, but a Simulation Team would not call them in. For example, your budget may not allow for a Sim Team, you may have a limited number of people who can participate, or you might have a lack of adequate equipment (no phones) to make a Sim Team work. Message Center forms could be used to provide the same information that a Sim Team caller would.

Message Center forms can be used if you are:

▶ Conducting a Basic Tabletop. In lieu of using a slide presentation to introduce injects, Message Center forms could be used.

SAMPLE MESSAGE CENTER FORM

Emergency Operating Center   Message Form

Date/Time _____ Person Receiving Call _____ Tracking # _____

Name of Caller/Their Location _____

Contact Information (voice, cell, and/or pager) _____

	IMPACTS			ASSIGNED TO EOC FUNCTION
SEVERITY RATING	**Life Safety**	**Facilities**	**Business**	Command
				Operations
CRITICAL <1 Hour				Logistics
IMPORTANT 1-4 Hours				Planning & Intelligence
DELAYED 5-8 Hours				Finance
				Communications

Message

_____
_____
_____
_____
_____
_____
_____
_____
_____
_____
_____

Message Validated **No Yes** By Whom? _____

Action Taken/Next Steps

_____
_____
_____
_____
_____
_____
_____
_____
_____
_____

Assignment Log/Closing/Re-Opening Information

Event Assigned To	
Event Closed: Date, Time, by Whom	
Event Re-Opened: Date, Time, by Whom	

► Conducting an Advanced Tabletop. The Simulation Team would be available to respond to the inject, but they would not be calling in the injects to the players.

► Conducting a Functional exercise. Even though a Functional exercise is a highly evolved exercise, for a variety of reasons, you may not want the Simulation Team to call in the injects. For example:

▷ You may have a relatively new team of players and don't want to overwhelm them.

▷ Your team may be fairly unsure of themselves and want to progress slowly from Advanced tabletop towards a Functional exercise. They may not be ready to accept inbound calls, but are ready to call their responses back.

▷ You lack a Message Center, or all the Message Center participants are brand new, or you've never had a Message Center before and this is your first time.

▷ There may be a desire to focus solely on the resolution of the problem. How they are informed of the problem is not the issue.

When using a Message Center form, fill it out by taking the information from the exercise script and simply cutting and pasting it into the form. If a Simulation Team is available to take the calls (and respond back to the players), you can also drop in the phone number of the Simulation Team member assigned to that call. The form will look just like it was received by a very efficient Message Center in your EOC, and forwarded to the team assigned.

A sample Message Center form is shown on the previous page.

Exercise types and appropriate documents

The following table is a summary of which documents are likely to be helpful in all five-exercise types. (Any boxes identified as "maybe" will depend on the characteristics of the exercise – number of sites, number of people, length and complexity of exercise, budget, etc.)

DOCUMENTS SORTED BY EXERCISE TYPE

	ORIENTATION	DRILL	TABLETOP	FUNCTIONAL	FULL-SCALE
Participant evaluation	Yes	Yes	Yes	Yes	Yes
Document summary	Yes	Yes	Yes	Yes	Yes
Phone directory	No	No	No	Yes	Yes
Executive briefing	No	No	Maybe	Maybe	Maybe
Message Center form	No	No	Yes	Maybe	No*
Evaluator form	No	Maybe	Maybe	Yes	Yes
Controller form	No	Maybe	Maybe	Yes	Yes
Observer form	No	Maybe	Maybe	Yes	Yes

* In a full-scale exercise, the injects would not be submitted to players by handing them a filled-out Message Center form. The Message Center would receive an inject (usually from a Simulator's phone call) and create a form themselves.

Summary

These last remaining documents tie together the loose pieces of the exercise, and provide a complete package for the exercise experience. Although each is simple and straightforward, they are an important aspect of the exercise and should be thoughtfully crafted to achieve the maximum result.

CHAPTER 10

Bringing it all together – the exercise team

After reading about all the prep work for your exercise, it's now time to introduce you to the cast of characters who will make it all happen on the day of the exercise. It may look like a large collection of people, but just like the Incident Command System[9], you only use what you need. For many exercises, your Exercise Team will likely be a small group; however, with a large exercise, you can have quite a party of people! The Exercise Team is comprised of the following positions:

- ▶ Exercise Management (Exercise Facilitator or Exercise Director).
- ▶ Simulation Team.
- ▶ Control Team.
- ▶ Evaluator.
- ▶ Exercise Assistants.
- ▶ Observer.
- ▶ Message Center.

Exercise management

There are two possible options for the role of exercise management:

- ▶ Exercise Facilitator.
- ▶ Exercise Director.

Exercise facilitator

This is a role that is used in the majority of exercises (see chart at the end of this chapter). Your organization may structure the position differently, however, the common responsibilities of the Exercise Facilitator include:

- ▶ Leading the design process. In most cases, it is likely that the Exer-

---

9   See glossary for ICS definition.

cise Facilitator also leads the exercise design process.

▶ Kicking off the exercise. Opens the exercise by reviewing the structure of the day, the exercise plan and scenario, and associated documents.

▶ Facilitating the exercise. Acts as the main (or only) Facilitator on the exercise day. Is responsible for the event from start to finish, including oversight of all players, and intervening (as necessary) during the "play time," observing and monitoring issues that need attention (such as injects gone awry or key injects being ignored).

▶ Managing the injects. Delivers the actual injects, or manages the Simulation Team who will.

▶ Conducting the debrief. Leads the team in the debrief session at the end.

▶ Developing the After-Action Report (AAR) (see Chapter 16). Prepares the AAR.

▶ Reviewing exercise findings. Prepares and delivers AAR and other reports to entities within the organization on the exercise findings. Reviews the project plan for remediation.

▶ Tracking progress of remediation (optional). May be tasked with following up on the project plan for remediation and charting progress.

Exercise director

The position of Exercise Director is often used only for larger Functional and Full-Scale exercises. In this role, the Director acts as an "overseer" of the entire event; the Simulation Team, Control Team, and evaluators report up to him or her. As the title implies, this is much like a movie director looking out over the enterprise. Ultimately, they are responsible for the same activities as the Exercise Facilitator. However, they may not personally perform those functions, they just need to ensure that they get done.

Simulation team

The Simulation Team (sometimes referred to as "the Sim Team") is the driver of the exercise, and can often make or break it. They will be deploying all of the injects and will become the "face of the exercise" to the players. No matter how great your exercise design, it's your Simulation Team that will make it shine (or not).

Simulation Team organization

If you have enough people, you may organize your Simulation Team members into three roles:

▶ Simulation Team Coordinator.

▶ Simulation Team member.

▶ Simulation Team Scribe.

Simulation Team Coordinator

In a larger exercise, it is necessary to have a Simulation Team Coordinator (STC) oversee the Simulation room and the activities in it. The responsibilities of the STC are to:

▶ Serve as the eyes and ears of the Exercise Facilitator/Director.

▶ Connect the Simulation Team to the Controllers.

▶ Assist the Simulation Team in developing responses, making up spontaneous injects, and providing general coaching help.

▶ Monitor the flow of the injects and keep the Sim Team on track.

▶ Serve as the Simulation Team contact point-person if something needs to be followed up on, an inject needs to be "righted," or an inject needs to be re-delivered.

▶ Attend the pre-exercise briefing(s), the exercise, and any post-exercise review meetings.

Simulation Team member

A Simulation Team member has the following responsibilities:

▶ Knowing and understanding the exercise plan.

▶ Knowing and understanding the exercise injects.

▶ Knowing and understanding the two main responsibilities of the Sim Team:

▷ Playing the "outside world."

> ▷ Knowing and understanding their assigned injects, and delivering them on time.
▶ Knowing the exercise timeline and story progression. In other words, knowing where the exercise is going.
▶ Knowing the resources available to them.
▶ Following instructions from Sim Coordinator (if present).
▶ Providing realistic time frames to players.
▶ Developing realistic spontaneous injects.
▶ Attending the pre-exercise briefing(s), the exercise, and any post-exercise review meetings.

Simulation Team Scribe

The Simulation Team Scribe has the following responsibilities:
▶ Knowing and understanding the exercise plan.
▶ Knowing the exercise timeline and story progression. In other words, knowing where the exercise is going.
▶ Scribing facts as requested by the Coordinator or Sim Team members.
▶ Attending the pre-exercise briefing(s), the exercise, and any post-exercise review meetings.

What makes a good simulation team participant?

While many people can be a Sim Team member, an outstanding Simulator will have the following qualities:
▶ Have a good overall knowledge of the company. The more they understand the organization, the better Simulator they will be.
▶ Have a good knowledge of specific departments that are being exercised. This is critical when exercising groups such as Facilities, IT, or critical lines of business. You just can't make those things up.
▶ Possess a good attitude and be a team player. Ideally they will be creative; if they have good acting skills, that's a plus! (Although you may find, as I have, that after a few minutes, even the most shy folks really get into the role.)

▶ Produce "credible scenarios" and yet stay on course with the exercise plan.

Design Team members make great Simulation Team members. Think about it: they know the exercise intimately and are already fully engaged in the process. Participating on the Simulation Team allows them to see their work all the way to fruition.

Simulation Team logistics

So how many Sim Team members do you need? That's a good question, and one which can be answered with a little math. Generally speaking, for every one inject the Sim Team sends inbound to the EOC, roughly one or two outbound calls will come back to the Sim Team. Using that guideline, you can get some idea of the traffic the team is likely to receive during the exercise based on how many injects you have. You will also need to consider the calls that will be delivered to them acting as the "outside world." My experience has taught me that for between 75 and 100 injects, an ideal Sim Team would be comprised of ten people. You may find that if you have fewer Simulators, they get too busy and can't keep on top of everything; on the other hand, too many Simulators may cause confusion over who is doing what.

Where do you put your Simulation Team? Should they be centralized in one room or dispersed throughout your EOC? In my experience, it is far better to have them all together in one room. This allows them to hear what each other is saying and follow the progression of the exercise. It also gives you a lot more control to have a centralized team. Having said that, space and telephony constraints may dictate the need to have a dispersed team. If that is the case, communication between and among team members will be critical. An Instant Messaging system or Google Word documents that can be shared as a status board can help all keep their stories straight and keep them connected.

Delivering and receiving calls

There are two rules about initiating any call or conversation:

▶ When starting the delivery of any call, *ALWAYS* start the phone message with the phrase, "This is an exercise message." It is possible that you may misdial the number and tell some unsuspecting person about the horrible thing that has just happened. Starting with "This is an exercise message" gets everyone on the same page right off the bat, and can avoid creating another War of the Worlds scenario!

▶ When picking up the phone, *ALWAYS* answer the phone with "May I help you?" You have no idea who the person on the other end is looking for. They could be calling back regarding an inject or they could be expecting you to play someone in the "outside world." If they start rambling, or if you are not sure who or what they are looking for, stop them right away and say, "Who are you looking for?" They should be able to respond with something like, "I am looking for John's Computer Service." You can then reply, "Hi, this is John's; how can I help you?" This quickly gets everyone on track and the call is off on a good foot.

The "Golden Rule," simulation style

Going back to the War of the Worlds scenario, I have one golden rule in the art of simulation: *NO MARTIAN LANDINGS!* What the heck does that mean? It is meant as a reminder to the Simulation Team to stay in line with the exercise flow, narrative, and injects. I have found that occasionally the Sim Team really gets into this world they are creating – the next thing you know, they are adding in unexpected situations and things that we didn't agree to, like a power outage, or an additional dead employee, or a second explosion. Anything that varies from the overall direction of the exercise needs to be cleared by the Exercise Facilitator. So, please – no Martians!

Simulation room set-up

Ideally, the Sim Team room should be near the exercise but completely separate, and it must be far enough away so the team players can't hear the Simulators. In other words, a shared wall would not be the best thing.

It is important to have the following:

▶ Adequately sized room and wall space. A U-shaped table is a great room layout. This allows the Coordinator to "walk the room" in the middle so she or he can eavesdrop on the calls and keep track of the action.

▶ Sufficient landline phones. Each Sim Team member must have their own phone. Ideally, there should be a hold button, but no voicemail, and the phones should not "roll" to each other. As discussed in Chapter 9, cell phones are not ideal. Remember that batteries can die, reception can be shaky, and lost calls happen on even the most "on" network. Providing the Simulator with a landline avoids those problems. In addition, whether using a company cell phone or a personal one, the Sim Team member may receive non-exercise calls, which would disrupt the exercise.

▶ White boards or flip charts for scribes to note the current status, important spontaneous injects, or new data from the players.

SIMULATION ROOM SET-UP

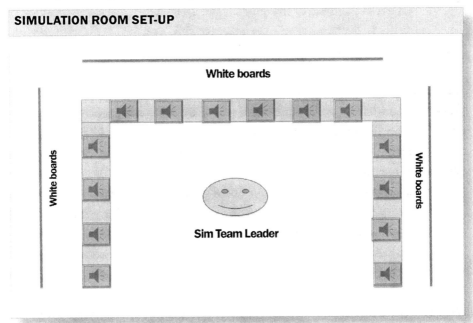

Control Team

A Control Team is most commonly used for larger Functional and Full-scale exercises. As the exercise increases in complexity, size, and scope, it is impossible for the Facilitator to be everywhere, monitoring, and managing the process; at that point, a Control Team is added to the mix. The Control Team is composed of two roles:

▶ Lead Controller (in large exercises).

▶ Controller.

Lead Controller

In a larger exercise it is often necessary to have a Lead Controller to oversee multiple Controllers.

▶ Serves as the eyes and ears of the exercise Facilitator/Director.

▶ Oversees the Controllers in the exercise.

▶ Monitors the overall performance of the exercise and the players.

▶ Manages the Controllers; reports issues and concerns to either the Exercise Facilitator/Director and/or Simulation Team Coordinator.

▶ Attends the pre-exercise briefing(s), the exercise, and any post-exercise review meetings.

Controller

▶ Reports any problems or issues that may arise concerning departure from the exercise plan or injects to the Lead Controller (if present). These include issues that could interfere with the exercise progress or exercise realism.

▶ Monitors player actions and notes observations. If this is a combined role of Controller and Evaluator (see Evaluator section), they will need to not only oversee inject management, but also provide overall feedback on the team performance. It can be challenging to be performing both hands-on management tasks while looking at a situation with an evaluator's eye.

▶ Monitors injects to ensure that the exercise is moving forward as planned.

▶ Tracks assigned key injects. (See "Tracking key injects" section for tips.)

▶ Works with the Simulation Team to develop spontaneous injects as needed.

▶ Records responses of players and maintain logs and forms.

▶ Attends the pre-exercise briefing(s), the exercise, and any post-exercise review meetings.

Evaluators

As the title implies, the Evaluator role performs the primary evaluation job of the exercise. In exercises where you are using Controllers, this function can often be fulfilled by that Controller role. However, in large exercises with many moving parts, you might need a separate Evaluator role. The Evaluator role has the following responsibilities:

▶ Understands the role of the team that he or she is assigned to evaluate.

▶ Knows and understands the exercise plan.

▶ Knows and understands the exercise injects.

▶ Works with Controllers to monitor "key injects" and provide feedback until they are successfully resolved.

▶ Knows the exercise timeline and story progression, in other words, where the exercise is going.

▶ Provides feedback to the Controllers and Simulation Team on their assigned teams' activities.

▶ Provides observant and objective observations.

▶ Reports to the Lead Controller.

▶ Attends the pre-exercise briefing(s), the exercise, and any post-exercise review meetings.

Exercise Assistants

Exercise Assistants are most often used in large exercises and provide another valuable set of hands to perform tasks during the exercise (if you have the budget, an assistant is useful in a smaller exercise as well). Some of the activities you might assign an assistant include:

▶ Play any audio-visual tools as in noted in the exercise script.

▶ Hand out any paper materials, including the exercise plan, any news stories "pulled from the web," or the participant evaluations.

▶ Make phone calls on behalf of the exercise Facilitator to check in with other locations, the Simulation Team, or others as necessary.

▶ Check in with the Facilitator frequently.

▶ Keep the exercise clock set to "exercise time" (if you have changed the time in the exercise plan), and ask everyone to reset their watches to exercise time.

▶ Assist with the debriefing session by scribing the debrief notes.

▶ Collecting the evaluation and observation forms.

Observers

The group of eyes I refer to as "observers" are not formal evaluators. Some organizations are required to have a "neutral third party," if you will, to observe the action. For example, a utility company may be required to have a representative from the Utility Commission present, or an auditor may need or want to attend to see how a financial company's response program has progressed.

However, an observer with no focus – nothing specific to do, just "observe" – can be a problem. They can wander around, get distracted, and start engaging other observers in conversation – or even the players. In addition to instructing them to not interact with the players, I always give observers a "job." Unless there are special circumstances, I require them to complete an evaluator form, and note their responses to the two major questions:

1. What worked in this exercise?
2. What needs improvement?

Should you assign them to a team, or do you let them roam? That can be your call, depending on your circumstances or the political climate of your organization. Either way, let them know that they are on the hook to provide you written feedback at the end of the exercise, clearly noting their observations.

Message center

If you are doing an Incident Management Team exercise that involves the activation of their EOC (Emergency Operations Center), you might need to have a Message Center staff (with or without "runners"). The Message Center will be your "switchboard," fielding phone calls, filling out Message Center forms (see Chapter 18), and routing the injects to the appropriate team or person. They may also be called on to track calls and follow up on them.

The Message Center may also have some people identified as "runners," who will use "sneaker-net" (i.e., walking around) to get information from one team to another, or to sweep the team's inboxes for completed forms.

Tracking key injects

There may be multiple positions tracking your "key injects" – observer, controller, evaluator, you – or just one of those roles. Regardless of how many people are on the lookout for them, here are a few suggestions on how to track them:

▶ Each key inject should be assigned to a specific person, who will follow their progress.

▶ The Observer/Controller/Evaluator should note on their observation form how the inject was handled.

▶ When a key inject is due to be delivered, stand near the intake phones to note how it is being handled as it comes in. Then, follow it around until it is resolved.

▶ Take note of how it is being handled. Is someone working on it, actively trying to get it resolved? Or is it just sitting there, unnoticed and unaddressed?

▷ If it's being worked on, take notes as to how it's being resolved.

▷ If it's being ignored, alert the Sim Team. They can call in the inject again – and again, and again – until it has been addressed properly.

▶ Check in with Sim Team for their feedback.

Orientation sessions – Sim Team, Evaluators, Controllers

A solid orientation will take you about two hours. The good news is that you can probably combine the Sim Team, Evaluator, and Controller sessions together, covering many of the same points across the roles. Here is a possible agenda to cover information applicable to all:

▶ Review roles and responsibilities.

▶ Review the exercise plan, overall injects, and key injects.

▶ Review any specific forms you are to use in the course of the exercise.

▶ Plot strategy for escalation of issues.

▶ Complete written evaluation at the end.

Note: Remind everyone to arrive at least 30 minutes before the start of the exercise on exercise day. This allows them plenty of time to get settled in and set up before the exercise begins.

Key points to emphasize – Sim Team

In addition to providing your Simulators with any necessary background information they will need to play their role, and reminding them they may be called upon to act as Sim Team Scribe, you should cover the following topics.

Inject delivery

▶ It is important to deliver the inject at the stated time. Although most injects are not so time-sensitive that being a few minutes off will result in the crashing failure of your exercise, the exercise can get bogged down if someone is chronically late delivering every inject.

▶ Develop a list of additional caller names in advance.

▶ Stay in line with the exercise script and objectives.

▶ Note any "key" injects you have been assigned. Your job is to keep them alive until resolved properly.

Organization

▶ Stay organized. Find a way to keep control over the exercise plan(s) and injects, such as using a binder or clipboard.

▶ Highlight your assigned injects and make sure you are clear about it, including the intent of the inject, how to deliver it, and your ability to answer any corresponding questions.

▶ Keep notes on what you said and the caller's response. Remembering all of these made-up stories is difficult; don't rely on your memory afterwards. Truth is easy to remember, lies not so much!

Acting skills

▶ React convincingly to the inject recipients' comments.

▶ Respond to a participant's requests/actions and repeat information if asked.

▶ Confer with others. If you need help in developing a response, put the caller on hold, consult with your teammates (and the Coordinator, if present), and then respond. You are surrounded by lots of people who can help you craft a good story.

Working with the rest of the team

▶ Be sure to keep the Sim Team Coordinator informed of any spontaneous stories that you created, or any emerging issues that may have come up in your calls.

▶ Keep Sim Team Scribe (if present) informed of impromptu stories.

Your health

▶ Pace yourself. This can be very tiring. It's a lot of fun, yes, but draining.

▶ Stay hydrated by drinking lots of fluids. This will also help avoid losing your voice.

Key points to emphasize – Control Team

▶ Review individual Control Team assignments. Become familiar with which team or group each Controller is assigned to oversee.

▶ Determine management of key injects. Develop approach if team fails to respond appropriately.

Key points to emphasize - Evaluator

It is important to emphasize some particular points in the Evaluator orientation.

The evaluation process:
- ▶ You are monitoring exercise play and relating it to the exercise objectives and expected outcomes. Evaluate <u>actions</u>, not <u>people</u>.
- ▶ Determine if objectives and related actions are met.
- ▶ Track key injects and report findings.
- ▶ Record findings on Evaluator form.

What evaluation methods should you employ?
- ▶ Observe participants.
- ▶ Look at situation boards and reporting forms.
- ▶ Look at any reports.
- ▶ Talk with participants to ensure clarity.
- ▶ Attend briefings.
- ▶ Be a "fly on the wall" to listen into conversations and informal briefings.

"Teachable moments"

In any exercise, there will be "teachable moments." These are moments when you see the team struggling, and you possess information that could move them farther along if only you would share it. Of course, you could withhold that information and just let them hit the wall – that's one type of exercise learning. However, another way to approach this situation is to provide just enough information to get them unstuck, then stand back and watch them go on their way again. Why would you chose this approach? Shouldn't you wait for them to find their way again? After all, aren't they supposed to learn from this experience?

Yes, you want them to learn, but look at it this way: You don't have exercises very often. If you could provide them some basic information or a moment of reflection that allows them to get "unstuck," they actually have a better chance of going farther in the exercise and learn more. I tell my Controllers and Evaluators that if they see the players struggling, not able to move forward, they have permission to try to "unstick" them by providing some data or asking a pointed question that may help them on their way.

The cast of characters

Now that we have reviewed all of the different characters and their roles, the following chart denotes who you are likely to need for each type of exercise.

THE CAST OF CHARACTERS						
POSITION	**ORIEN-TATION**	**DRILL**	**TABLETOP**	**FUNCTIONAL**	**FULL-SCALE**	**MULTIPLE SITES**
Exercise Facilitator	Yes	Yes	Yes	Yes	No	Yes, plus Facilitator at other sites
Exercise Director	No	No	No	No	Yes	Yes (at primary site)
Simulation Team	No	No	Basic – no Advanced – yes	Yes	Yes	Yes
Control Team	No	Maybe	No	Yes; may combine with Evaluator role	Yes	Yes; may combine with Evaluator role
Evaluator	No	Maybe	Yes	Yes; may combine with Controller role	Yes	Yes; may combine with Controller role
Observer	Maybe	Maybe	Maybe	Maybe	Maybe	Maybe
Exercise Assistant(s)	Maybe	Maybe	Maybe	Maybe	Maybe	Maybe

Any boxes identified as "maybe" will depend on the characteristics of the exercise – number of sites, number of people, length and complexity of exercise, budget, etc.

Sample organizational charts

Here are four different versions of how an Exercise Team organizational chart might look like.

Orientation exercise or Basic Tabletop

For an Orientation or Basic Tabletop exercise, it's likely that the exercise "team" will be one member – the Facilitator. If Assistants are available and/or Observers will be present, they should report to the Facilitator.

Advanced Tabletop

An Advanced Tabletop exercise would also have a Simulation Team, which would report to the Facilitator. If Assistants are available and/or Observers will

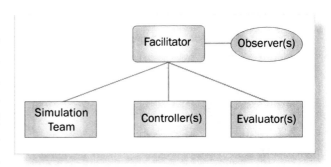

be present, they, too, should report to the Facilitator.

Functional Exercise

With more players, the Functional Exercise team is comprised of the Exercise Facilitator, a Simulation Team and Evaluator/Controllers. The Sim Team, Evalua-

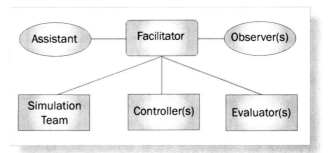

tor/Controller and any observers report to the Facilitator, along with any Assistants and/or Observers.

Full-Scale Exercise

A Full-Scale Exercise has the most exercise team members; the organization usually looks like the diagram on the right.

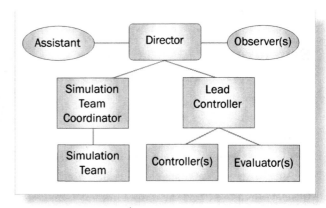

Summary

The exercise team is the group in charge of taking your carefully crafted exercise and delivering it to the players. Their role is critical to the success of your exercise. Carefully select, train, and coach these individuals to ensure that they will help you achieve the goals and objectives of the exercise.

CHAPTER 11

Finally – the big day arrives: Managing the exercise day

You've made it! Give yourself a hand for doing all the hard work to get to this point – your big day. The goal of this chapter is to carefully examine the final exercise activities, from a few days before the exercise to executing the exercise event itself.

Planning your time – before the big day

The design is done, the writing is completed, the meetings are over, and now your "exercise baby" is about to be born. What should you be doing and thinking about leading up to the start of the exercise? Just like all of the planning to this point, the devil is in the details.

A few days before

Reminders

This is a good time to reconnect with the exercise team. There may have been a relatively long gap between the last design meeting and the actual exercise day; now is when they should really be paying attention to your emails and missives. What "memory jogs" should you give them? What needs prompting at this point?

▶ It is always good to remind all exercise participants about the agenda, goals, and objectives. This will help them focus on the tasks at hand in advance and prompt them to possibly do some preparation. (If you haven't created a separate document with just these sections, simply take your exercise plan and delete everything except the agenda, goals, and objectives.)

▶ If you need them to bring something specific with them, this is the time to ask/remind them of what they should have with them or have immediate access to – anything they might need in order to do their assigned task. This could include such items as laptops, individual BCP documents, floor plans, mobile phones, maps, or other important pieces of equipment or information.

Training

The day or two before the exercise is a good time to do any of the required training that is necessary for the exercise team. One of the advantages to having an exercise in the private sector is that most organizations have very few activations on an annual basis. Of course, one of the disadvantages is that most organizations have very few activations on an annual basis... A double-edged sword! If you want you the exercise to run smoothly and have your best chance for players get the most out of the experience, some advance training of the exercise team can bring them up to a "level playing field" from the start of the exercise.

There are three types of training that you might need to conduct:
▶ Simulation Team / Controllers / Evaluators / Observers.
▶ Message Center.
▶ Player training.

Simulation Team / Controllers / Evaluators / Observers

This orientation training is discussed in the Chapter 10. It is critical that all members of the exercise team know their individual roles and the responsibilities of that role – and are comfortable with them from the start.

Message Center

If you are doing an Incident Management Team exercise that involves the activation of their EOC (Emergency Operations Center), you might need to do some Message Center training. Ideally, they will have incorporated the Message Center concept into their EOC. Even if they have, and especially if they don't activate often, it is important to cover the following topics with the Message Center operators and runners:

▶ Answering the phone.

▶ Filling out the Message Center form.

▶ Routing the calls. (It is often helpful to provide examples of calls and where they would go.)

▶ Reviewing the roles and responsibilities of each team. (This will also help them route the calls properly.)

▶ Tracking calls and following up with them.

▶ Ensuring all calls are answered and dealt with.

Player training

The players themselves often benefit from training a few days before the exercise as well. At this point they are usually highly receptive to the information, and by having a quick refresher before the exercise, it is more likely they will "hit the ground running" and make greater strides in the exercise than if they had no training. The topics to cover depend, of course, on what type of exercise you are conducting. However, here is a broad range of topics to choose from:

▶ Basic overview of the team, including roles and responsibilities.

▶ Review of how the EOC operates.

▶ Discussion of how calls are answered, logged, and tracked.

▶ Review of all forms they will encounter through the exercise.

▶ Outline of the documentation to be included on status boards.

▶ Overview of reports and briefings that may occur during the exercise.

▶ Review of how to develop an Incident Action Plan and how to run an IAP meeting.

The day before

The day before the exercise, I always to like to check over everything **one more time.** That might sound a bit odd – after all, you have probably looked at it a zillion times already – but I find great comfort knowing I have checked it all once again and am certain everything is "good to go." Here's a short list of things you may want to review **one more time:**

▶ Recheck the flow of the day, the narrative, the agenda, and the key inputs.

▶ Reconfirm all of the logistics, including meeting room set-up and catering.

▶ Ensure that all materials have been printed and are correct (pages in the right order and oriented the same way, the correct documents ready to be given to the correct people, etc.).

> One critical thing to keep in your mind at all times – you are the **"holder of the exercise vision."** You need to know this thing backwards and forwards, and have a **perfectly** clear idea of where it is going at all times.

Room set-up

NOTE: If it's at all possible, try to set up the room the day before. If anything is amiss, you'll be grateful for the extra time to fix it.

Most organizations conduct their exercises in a "standard" conference room. Few companies have the luxury of a "hot" EOC, always set up and able to be used at a moment's notice. It is, therefore, always preferable to do the room set-up the day before the exercise. This prevents those last-minute issues from driving you over the edge. It also allows you to get a better night's rest before the exercise! Here is a short list of items to consider when doing the room set-up:

▶ Validate the equipment list, and ensure everything was ordered and is now available.

▶ Prepare any necessary identifying directional signs.

▶ Identify the location of the closest copier and fax machine. Ensure they work properly.

▶ If using phones, install and test all of the lines and devices. (Yes, every line and every device.)

▶ Ensure phone numbers in the phone directory are mapped to the correct device.

▶ If conducting any audio-conference briefings (for example, an Executive or multi-site briefing), ensure that an appropriate speakerphone is

available and works properly.
▶ Prepare a sign-in table. (Pre-printed sign-in sheets are not only help-ful, they provide a good audit trail).
▶ Set out table tent signage for team(s) and/or individual seating.
▶ Ensure there are sufficient flip charts, markers, and tape available for use as status boards.
▶ Verify all equipment/devices that will be used to play any audio-visual broadcasts (audio) or display visual presentations (slides or video) are working properly.
▶ Make sure the A-V materials can be seen or heard from every position in the room.
  ▷ If that's not possible due to the room size or layout, try to find a place that can accommodate the most number of players.
▶ Ensure that you have all necessary office supplies available.
▶ Have a camera available. Make sure the batteries are fresh and there is room on the memory card for a substantial number of pictures.
▶ If you will be holding a mock press conference, have a video camera set up in an appropriate place (or ready to be set up at the right time). Make sure the batteries are fresh and there is room on the memory card or tape to last through the scheduled time.

Planning your time – the big day

A few hours before the start

After all of your great planning, care, and preparation you are now ready to go!
▶ Plan to arrive at the exercise site **at least** one hour before the first agenda item is due to start. Again, this gives you the luxury of time to check and double-check, and fix any problems that you missed earlier.
▶ For larger exercises or multiple-site exercises, if at all possible, plan on having an assistant who can be another resource for you.
▶ Make sure you have multiple ways of being reached during the exer-cise. At a minimum, this should include a reliable mobile phone with a

fully charged battery, and landline numbers that you will be near.

▶ Make sure all of the exercise team has checked in: Simulators, Observers, Controllers and/or Evaluators. If anyone has not shown up and your are short a number of bodies, be prepared to go to "Plan B."

"Plan B"

Robert Burns' old saying, "the best laid plans of mice and men oft' go astray," could have been said instead by a good continuity planner. Always expect the unexpected. Just because you think you've done all you can for the exercise day to be perfect, something can still go askew. In other words, always have a "Plan B," especially when it comes to having the right amount of people.

▶ If Evaluators/Controllers/Observers don't show up:

▷ Call others in to help. This works for an Evaluator role in particular.

▷ Have Evaluators double-up who they are tasked with watching.

▶ If Simulation Team members don't show up:

▷ Have the rest of the Sim Team do double-duty – spread out the injects among those who are there.

▷ Delete the less important injects.

▷ Combine several injects together.

▷ Remind the rest of the Simulation Team to make sure that the phone gets answered.

Who's doing what? Exercise team tasks

So who's actually doing what on the exercise day?

Exercise Assistant tasks

▶ Makes sure the room clocks are set to exercise time (if the exercise time is different from the "real time").

▷ Asks everyone to reset their watches to exercise time or remove them to avoid confusion.

▶ Checks in with facilitator frequently.

▶ Plays any media as needed: video, radio broadcast, etc.
▶ Hands out any pertinent documents.
▶ Scribes notes during the debriefing.
▶ Helps the facilitator with other tasks that will undoubtedly crop up.

Simulation Team reminders

The Simulation Team is the engine that drives the exercise. It is now up to them to deliver. The Simulation Team should:

▶ Deliver injects on time.
▶ Be efficient when delivering injects. Ideally, you want a relatively concise and to-the-point delivery.
  ▷ Remind them that while they are talking on the phone, their number is busy and they can't be reached.
▶ Follow-up on calls not being returned or issues not being addressed.
▶ Keep all fellow Simulation Team members, Simulation Team Coordinator, and the exercise Facilitator informed of any issues or potential problems.
▶ Keep the Simulation Team Scribe informed or use a status board to note big issues that arise in the exercise.

Evaluator/Controller/Observer reminders

The Evaluator/Controller/Observer is another set of eyes and ears for you, and helps to keep the Facilitator and Simulation Team informed of what they are hearing and seeing.

▶ The three most important activities: Listen, follow, and pay attention.
▶ Keep the facilitator informed of what's going on.
▶ Keep notes on the evaluator/observer/controller form.

Starting line – the exercise briefing

"Rules of engagement"

Once the players have assembled and the time has come to begin the exercise, before diving into the exercise plan, it's a good idea to review some "rules of engagement." This is especially advised if it is an Orientation exercise and, therefore, a new situation for the players. Without some basic guidelines, the day could easily go sideways.

Remind the players that the purpose of the exercise is to:

▶ Discuss how they would handle the incident and talk through the various options in response.

▶ Explore areas for improvement in the current process and note those ideas.

Ask them to keep the following things in mind:

▶ Don't fight the narrative(s). They have been designed to help practice and look at current processes.

▶ Imagine that this has really happened, rather than it "could happen."

▶ This is a learning experience – there are no grades or pass/fail. Mistakes will happen, they are expected, and we encourage them! (It's better to make them in an exercise than during the real thing.)

Plan briefing

Once the ground rules have been established, it's time to distribute the exercise plan to all players and review the entire document with them.

▶ Thoroughly review the players' instructions, the plan, and the narrative. It is important that players clearly understand all the information.

  ▷ If the plan was distributed in advance, it is important to still review the document with them. Just because you gave it out in advance doesn't mean that they read it, or fully understood it.

▶ If a Simulation Team will be used, review the phone directory, how it is used, and the role of the Simulation Team. This is especially critical for the players if a Sim Team is a new concept for them.

  ▷ If you discover that players are not clear once the exercise starts, you may want to make a room-wide announcement to ensure that the Simulation Team and phone directory are being used correctly.

At the conclusion of the exercise briefing, I always like to give the participants a few minutes to get in place and "ground" themselves before starting to deliver the injects.

Ready, set, go...

If you are using an audio-visual broadcast or video, it is helpful to start the exercise with those aids in order to impart realism and set the tone. This often marks the "emotional start" to the exercise.

As the exercise Facilitator, once the exercise begins, you need to *float*. Don't get into active problem-solving if you can avoid it. If you have Controllers or Evaluators, delegate issues when possible and move on. Just like the old surfer saying, it is always better to "hang loose."

At this point, your real work is already done. You just need to float and monitor, and try to keep everyone on an even keel. Of course, you will probably want to keep your fingers crossed – and maybe get out the rabbit's foot, too – because once it starts, it's the player's exercise, and much of it is out of your control.

Simulation Team reminders

As an exercise Facilitator, in addition to reminding them of their responsibilities (see Chapter 10, Exercise Team), I like to check in with the Sim Team and remind them to:

- ▶ Relax and have fun. Stay loose and be flexible.
- ▶ Stay in role.
  - ▷ On the other hand, don't go too crazy. Remember: No Martian landings, please!
- ▶ Check with the Exercise Facilitator, Assistant, or Simulation Team Coordinators if they have any questions.

Evaluator/Controller/Observer reminders

Ensure that the Evaluator/Controller/Observer(s) are in position and remind them to:

- ▶ "Be a fly on the wall."
- ▶ Observe participants in the key roles. Insert your head into conversations to listen.
- ▶ Look at situation boards and forms.
- ▶ Look at reports.

▶ Attend briefings.

▶ Talk with participants as appropriate.

▶ If acting as a Controller, work with the injects as you were instructed to do. This could include inserting injects and/or following them.

▶ Follow the "key" injects around the room as they come in to see how they are managed.

▶ Interact with exercise players if "teachable moments" occur.

Observing exercise action

During an exercise, injects are delivered to the players using a variety of methods. The players then assess the inject and develop a response to the information in it. A feedback loop naturally occurs from observing the player response from inject delivery, to situation assessment, to response.

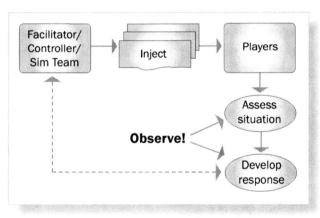

Mid-point check – everything okay?

Exercise pacing

As you were readying your inject document (see Chapter 6), the last thing you did was to sequence and time the injects over the course of the exercise "play time." Now that it's exercise day, when do you start delivering those injects? When do you stop? How do you adjust if the exercise seems like it's going too fast or too slow?

The question of when to start delivering injects depends on what your players normally do at the beginning of the exercise. Do they typically start with an Incident Action Planning (IAP) session? Is there some other activity they do first? Based on how your team operates, you have the option of starting the injects during that planning activity or after it has concluded. By and large, when I'm working with more experienced players, I will start delivering injects while the planning activity is going on. In your situation, you may want to give them a few minutes to "get their feet under them."

Once the injects begin, be aware of how the participants are doing. Are they coping well? Overwhelmed? Underwhelmed? Although your injects are already timed, you can, of course, modulate the flow based on your observations. Too harried? Slow it down a bit. Bored? Speed them up and encourage the Sim Team to think of spontaneous injects that would keep them engaged.

As the exercise unfolds, remember our basic question, *Why are we doing this exercise?* In all likelihood, the answer is not "to overwhelm the participants." You will find that for the players, there is sometimes a fine line between their being bored and running 500 miles an hour. Both situations could have them wanting to run out of the room screaming. Make sure the injects are challenging for the players, but don't send them over the edge. Be on the alert for signs of obvious frustration among the players. If you overhear griping or complaining during the exercise, speak to them and see if you can resolve their concerns then and there.

What should you be doing while the players are playing?

During the entire exercise, your task is to:

▶ Pay attention, observe, float around.
▶ Observe player behavior.
▶ Eavesdrop on calls and conversations.
▶ Check in with Evaluators/Observers/Controllers.
▶ Check in with the Simulation Team.
> ▷ If you (or a Controller) hears something that you think might "throw" the Simulation Team off, go tell them what is coming and help them with a response.
> ▷ Keep the Sim Team posted on what is going on "out there" and possible ways to respond. They're in the Sim room – you are their eyes and ears!

    ▷ Check their progress, help plot responses, or give encouragement.
- If it's possible, take lots of photos. You will likely be able to catch moments that no one else will.
- Capture your observations in writing during the exercise. Even a short cryptic note will help you remember the thought when you sit down to write your report.

How to handle an exercise that's going "sideways"

An exercise going "sideways" is one that's going awry for one reason or another. There are a variety of ways that this can happen – sometimes players get hung up about an issue, they get stuck on a situation, they simply hit the wall. Whatever the reason, you need to get it headed in the right direction again.

One of the ways to lessen this likelihood, is for you (as Facilitator) to constantly be in motion around the exercise – "floating" – listening, stepping in and helping where appropriate. Constantly ask our basic question, *Why are we doing this exercise?* You want to challenge the team, but you do not want them to be needlessly frustrated. By walking around and observing the action, you can be on the lookout for situations that seem like they're headed the wrong way, conversations that don't seem to fit with the event, or signs of an overactive imagination.

Your job as a Facilitator (or, if instructed, as the Controller/Evaluator) is to assist and support the team where possible, with the goal of moving the exercise forward to meet the goals and objectives.

With those thoughts in mind, if you overhear something that you know is not true, was misconstrued, or otherwise doesn't fit with what you know about the exercise, you have a couple of options to shift it. Which you choose will depend on the exercise, the company culture, and the demeanor of the players:
- Step in and correct it at the moment.
  - ▷ Point out the appropriate information on status boards, previous injects, or other places where the right information could be found. ("I can see on the status board that the power is still out on Main Street.")
  - ▷ Ask the player to call the Sim Team (as whichever entity would

know the proper response) to verify the information. ("If you call the power company, they can confirm if the power is up on Main Street yet.")

▶ Conversely, ask the Simulation Team to call in a correction to the player(s) who appear to be off-track. ("Just to confirm, it is a rumor that power is back up on Main Street.")

Almost at the finish line

Whew! What likely took several months to plan is – quite amazingly – over in just a few hours. The phones have stopped ringing, the Sim Team has delivered their last inject, the players have wrestled with their last request for "more laptops," the room has paper all over the place, and the exercise is now done. Hooray!

Well, hang on there, cowboy. Don't start celebrating yet, and certainly don't sit down to rest – you've still got things to do.

Exercise debrief

A critically important last piece still remains – the exercise debrief (or the "hotwash," as it's called in the public sector). The debrief sessions goals are to:

▶ Review and evaluate the exercise and the experience.
▶ Provide feedback regarding plans and performance.
▶ Review lessons learned from the exercise.

This is an absolutely critical activity. It is important to make sure that you assign someone to take good notes as you facilitate the debrief – it is exceedingly difficult to facilitate and scribe notes well at the same time. The information you get from the debrief, combined with the written evaluations, your observations, and the observations from the Controllers/Evaluators are a major portion of your after-action report. Besides providing valuable information for the exercise report, I often get many great gems from this session, fodder for the next exercise.

Debrief format

During the debrief, you are trying to get participants' reactions to the day's events. The usual format I use for the debrief is to ask for impressions and observations in the following order:

▶ The general audience.

▶ Team leaders, section chiefs, or business leaders.

▶ Exercise players.

▶ Incident Commander or person in charge.

Let everyone know the above sequence; this way, the participants understand the flow and if/when they may be called on specifically to respond. Especially inform team leaders or senior staff if they will be asked to share observations on behalf of their team so they may be prepared.

Debrief questions

Just asking, "What did you think of the exercise?" is a good way to be completely overwhelmed and have the debrief turn into a massive ball of chaos. Instead, I prefer to ask two basic questions. These questions provide a focus, while getting people to open up. Normally, they will probably get you 90% to 95% of the information you desire:

▶ "What worked in this experience?"

▶ "What didn't work?" (Alternately, you could phrase it as "What needs improvement?")

As mentioned above, start with the general audience. Encourage everyone to share their experiences and their key learnings. Move on to team leaders or business leaders (if using ICS, this would be section chiefs). Follow with the individual exercise teams, and end with the Incident Commander (or person in charge of the incident).

The debriefing should be quick and move along at a good pace, usually lasting no more than an hour. Things in particular to note include issues regarding:

▶ Communication.

▶ Command.

▶ Control.

▶ Coordination.

Debrief style – "Talk show host"

Not quite "Heeeeeeeeere's Johnny!" but I often do feel like a "talk show host" when I run the debrief this way. This style is large and inclusive. The Facilitator reviews the debrief basics, who speaks in what order, and then begins, drawing information out of the crowd by asking the first question and then waiting for the response.

I always start with the positive "What worked well in this exercise?" When that exploration has been exhausted, I move on to the "What needs improvement?" question. As mentioned before, I suggest having someone else be the scribe. If you can get two people to scribe the notes, even better. I find that with two people, I am likely to get 99% of the comments; with one person, I only get about 80% - sometimes less. The scribing can be done by taking notes on an easel in front of the group, or by using regular notepads while seated.

Debrief style – small groups

When the player population is quite large, it is often easier to use a small group format. In this style, the teams work together in their small groups to gather the same information. Have each team elect a scribe and a Facilitator (or assign the task to your Controller(s)/Evaluator(s)/Observer(s)); the Facilitator will ask the two basic questions. When done, reassemble in the large group, where each team reports out on two to four of their top responses for both "what worked" and "what needs improvement."

Although this format saves time and can accommodate a large team, I find that I don't get as many varied responses when done this way.

Regardless of which style you select, be sure to collect all of the scribes' notes at the end for your after action-report.

Written exercise evaluations

The last task of the day is to get the participants to fill out the written evaluations. This is another crucial piece of feedback. Many people feel more comfortable sharing written thoughts anonymously than they do sharing out loud in a group, so I don't provide a space for a name on the evaluation form.

I encourage you to spend time developing this tool so that you get out of it what you want to know. It can provide great feedback to you on the status of your program, plans, teams, and issues – or it can tell you a whole lot of nothing if a question is mis-asked or not asked at all. (Evaluation documents are discussed in Chapter 9.) Be sure to consider asking questions related to:

▶ Overall reaction to the exercise experience.

▶ Adequacy of the existing plan.

▶ Exercise itself.

▶ Ideas for further training and exercises.

▶ Suggestions for improvement.

Two important words – "Thank you"

Before you call it a day and let the participants go, you need to say a big "thank you" to everyone who made this possible. It may go without saying, but I'll say it anyway: the Exercise Team members (Simulation Team, Controllers/Evaluators/ Observers, design team, assistants) all need a big **THANK YOU** at the end. As the Facilitator, you definitely need to say this; hopefully, a senior management person will echo this, saying the final, important, "thank you" as well.

The party's over!

Check in with your teams

Even though everyone will be spreading to the winds after the exercise, before they go, gather together your exercise team members (Simulation Team / Evaluators / Controller / Observers) to capture some of their initial reactions to the exercise. They should have, of course, completed their own evaluations and observation documents, but it is great to get everyone together for a quick 20 minute check-in, and give some personal thank yous. They worked hard with you to make the day a big success; it's an ideal time to find out how it went from their perspective. They also might have some good ideas and suggestions for the development of the next exercise, or the program, the plan, or for team improvements.

Room clean-up

Be sure to allocate enough time and personnel to clean up the room properly.

▶ Determine what you want to save. Give clear instructions to your clean-up crew. Many documents can be used for writing the After-Action Report; in some cases, the documents may be used for audit purposes. (See Chapter 15 on what you may need to keep.) Don't forget things like:

▷ Message Center forms.

▷ Status board sheets.

▷ Staffing charts.

▷ Call logs.

▷ Sign-in sheets.

▶ Collect all exercise materials (plans, news releases, etc.) and ensure that they are properly destroyed (shredding is recommended to avoid "bad" information from falling into the wrong hands).

▶ Ensure all equipment is returned and packed up for use the next time.

▶ Collect all participant evaluations, evaluator forms, and sign-in sheets.

Exercise Team debrief

Lastly, we end this experience where we began – with your Exercise Team. Ideally, try to meet with the exercise Design Team no later than two weeks after the exercise (longer than this and memories start to fade). Going back full circle is a helpful experience as it allows you to really look at what happened in the exercise and compare them to what you thought might happen. This meeting can be relatively short (an hour or less) and it can help you collect process improvement points, ideas and thoughts for your next exercise, along with program and plan development ideas.

Congratulations! You made it! Now you can celebrate!

Summary

All of your careful planning has paid off. After all of that work, you complete the process by facilitating the exercise. Remember that when the exercise concludes, you aren't done yet. You need to facilitate a thoughtful debriefing session, ensure that good notes are taken and the exercise documents necessary to write the after action report are retained. Congratulations! You made it! Now you can celebrate!

CHAPTER 12

How to conduct an orientation exercise

Orientation exercises are a great way to introduce a new plan to a team, or a new team to a plan. There are several advantages to this type of exercise:

▶ Can be lower cost due to shorter development time and fewer resources needed to conduct.

▶ Can be developed quickly, usually in less than a month.

▶ Provides participants with a relatively easy way to validate the plan.

▶ Gets everyone oriented to the plan basics.

Orientation Exercise checklist

This checklist can be used as a guide and timeline for developing Orientation Exercises.

NOTE: Italicized sections are included as samples in the next section. Documents not included here can be found in Chapter 9, "Additional Documents."

ORIENTATION EXERCISE CHECKLIST		
ACTIVITY	DATE	ASSIGNED TO
Two months before		
☐ Select date and time for exercise.		
☐ Reserve room.		
☐ Send out a *"save the date"* communication (email, voicemail, fax, etc.) to the players.		
Six weeks before		
☐ Explore the question, *Why are we doing this exercise?* (See Chapter 4.)		
☐ Develop Document Summary form.		
☐ Develop the goal and objectives of the exercise.		

ORIENTATION EXERCISE CHECKLIST

ACTIVITY	DATE	ASSIGNED TO
☐ Validate goal and objectives with appropriate individuals; modify accordingly.		
Four weeks before		
☐ Send *exercise agenda* to players. Include goal, objectives, and agenda/timeline.		
☐ Develop complete *exercise plan*.		
☐ Three Weeks Before		
☐ Develop *slides* for exercise.		
☐ Develop participant evaluation.		
Two weeks before		
☐ Order catering for exercise (coffee, lunch, etc.). If ordering lunch, try to get a box lunch; this makes the food serving go much faster.		
☐ Order audio-visual equipment (LCD projector, flip charts, etc).		
One week before		
☐ Order printed materials (Exercise plan, Participant Evaluations, other documents as necessary).		
☐ Send follow-up email to players reminding them of the exercise. Include reminder of any items they may need to bring.		
Day before exercise		
☐ Set up room.		
☐ Verify proper functioning of all audio-visual equipment.		
☐ Set up "parking lots" (see Glossary).		
Exercise day		
☐ Conduct exercise.		
☐ Collect participant evaluations at the end.		
☐ Collect and properly destroy exercise materials after the exercise.		
No longer than two weeks AFTER exercise		
☐ Write After-Action Report (AAR).		
No longer than three weeks AFTER exercise		
☐ Distribute AAR.		

Orientation exercise – sample materials

Orientation exercises can stand alone, be combined with other training such as plan review, or be targeted for specific topics like the Incident Command System (ICS). These sample materials illustrate a combination ICS workshop and orientation exercise.

"Save the date" communication

"Please save the date for a very important training to be held on
<<exercise date and time>> to kick off the implementation of a
new emergency management system and plan here at <<company
name>>. You will be playing an important role in the system, and
your attendance at this important event is critical. Please mark
your calendar for <<date and time>>. The session will be held at the
<<meeting location>> and will be held for <<number>> hours. Additional information will be sent a few weeks prior to the session.
Thanks again – I look forward to seeing you on <<date>>"

Don't forget to ask all players to send an RSVP back to you. Silence does not always equal affirmation. If you get no response, follow up.

Document summary

For an Orientation Exercise, the most likely documents you will need are: Exercise Plan, exercise slides, participant evaluation. If you are conducting a workshop or training in conjunction with the Orientation exercise, you will also need workshop slides. A sample document summary format can be found in Chapter 9.

ORIENTAION EXERCISE DOCUMENT SUMMARY				
ITEMS NEEDED	PRINTING INSTRUCTIONS	DEVELOPMENT STATUS	WHO RECEIVES IT	DATE COMPLETED
Workshop slides	Color is nice but not required		Everyone	
Exercise Plan	B/W		Everyone	
Exercise slides	Do not print		No one	
Participant evaluation	B/W		Everyone	

Agenda
Exercise Agenda <<date>>

Goal

To orient the <<company name>> Incident Management Team (IMT) to the Incident Command System.

Objectives

▶ Review the Incident Command System (ICS).

▶ Review and validate the IMT organizational chart.

▶ Review and validate key aspects of the IMT plan.

▶ Review and validate the initial assessment process.

▶ Review IMT roles and responsibilities.

▶ Review the Incident Action Plan (IAP) process.

▶ Practice and refine team roles and processes through an orientation exercise.

Agenda

EXCERCISE AGENDA		
ACTIVITY	**TIME**	**DISCUSSION LEADER**
Welcome and Introductions	9:00 AM – 9:10 AM	J. Smith
▶ The Incident Command System (ICS) ▶ IMT Roles and Responsibilities ▶ Initial Assessment Team ▶ Incident Action Plan (IAP) Development	9:10 AM – 11:45 PM	R. Jones E. Charters E. Charters R. Jones
Lunch	11:45 AM – 12:30 PM	
Orientation Exercise	12:30 PM – 2:20 PM	R. Facilitator
Debrief	2:20 PM – 2:55 PM	R. Facilitator
Next steps	2:55 PM – 3:00 PM	J. Smith

Exercise plan

ICS workshop and orientation exercise <<date>>

1. *Exercise type and scope*

▶ Orientation Exercise.

▶ <<note who is playing>> is playing, all other departments and groups are simulated.

2. *Goal*

To orient the <<company name>> Incident Management Team (IMT) to the Incident Command System.

3. *Objectives*

▶ Review the Incident Command System (ICS).

▶ Review and validate the IMT organizational chart.

▶ Review and validate key aspects of the IMT plan.

▶ Review and validate the initial assessment process.

▶ Review IMT roles and responsibilities.

▶ Review the Incident Action Plan (IAP) process.

▶ Practice and refine team roles and processes through an orientation exercise.

4. *Agenda*

ICS WORKSHOP AND ORIENTATION EXERCISE AGENDA		
ACTIVITY	**TIME**	**DISCUSSION LEADER**
Welcome and Introductions	9:00 AM – 9:10 AM	J. Smith
▶ The Incident Command System (ICS) ▶ IMT Roles and Responsibilities ▶ Initial Assessment Team ▶ Incident Action Plan (IAP) Development	9:10 AM – 11:45 PM	R. Jones E. Charters E. Charters R. Jones
Lunch	11:45 AM – 12:30 PM	
Orientation Exercise	12:30 PM – 2:20 PM	R. Facilitator
Debrief	2:20 PM – 2:55 PM	R. Facilitator
Next steps	2:55 PM – 3:00 PM	J. Smith

5. Instructions to participants

▶ Exercises have the greatest value if they are treated as real. Stay in role the entire time.

▶ Don't just think about responding to what is coming at you – remember to keep one eye into the future and play the game of "what-if."

▶ As the exercise progresses, details may not be as complete as you would like. The value is in the process, the dialogue, and the experience. The design team has worked to make the situations as realistic as possible.

▶ You may only use what is in place as of today; if new equipment is being added next month, it is not in place and can't be used.

▶ Exercises are for learning; we expect mistakes. The goal is to develop the team and learn from the experience.

▶ In order to make this exercise work and to facilitate the learning process, a certain amount of "exercise magic" has been used. We ask you not to debate that something has happened, could have happened, or is available – it just is!

▶ Questions regarding the exercise should be directed to the exercise facilitator.

6. Evaluation

The exercise will be evaluated by use of participant written evaluations, the debrief session, and facilitators observations based on the objectives.

7. Exercise artificialities and assumptions

▶ All information in the narrative is to be considered valid.

▶ All information provided by the facilitator is to be considered valid.

▶ Don't assume anything else. All information can be verified by asking the facilitator.

8. Exercise narrative

The exercise narrative will be presented via slides.

Exercise slides

Fire!

- At 6:08 AM Monday, a fire broke out in <<location>>.
  - The fire spread quickly throughout the <<describe amount of space/floors>>.
  - Firefighters are pouring water onto the <<which floor>>.
  - Due to the amount of water being placed on the fire and electrocution risk to firefighters, power has been cut to the building.
    - This includes any UPS and generator support.
- The fire has now grown to a three-alarm blaze.

Floor Plan

It's Bad...

- The staff who were in the buildin the time of the fire have still been accounted for.
- Two firefighters have been killed.
- Your staff are being held back block from the building and will be granted access.
- The fire is being called "suspicio The local arson team and ATF being called in to investigate.
- You do not know the status of other building at this time.

Assessment

◆ Initial Assessment Team meets:
  - What is the level of this event?
  - Should the plan be activated?
  - Do you activate the IMT?
    ◆ Who should be called in?

Incident Action Plan Meeting

◆ Develop strategic objectives.
◆ Assign objectives to team or individual
  - Are adequate resources available?
◆ Determine Operational Period:
  - When does the team meet again?

Debrief

- What worked?
- What needs improvement?
- Next steps.

Participant evaluation

A sample participant evaluation can be found in Chapter 9.

Orientation Exercise timing guideline

The following is a guideline on how to conduct an Orientation Exercise using the exercise and slides included in this chapter. The agenda assumes the exercise runs from 12:30 PM to 3:00 PM.

ORIENTATION EXERCISE ACTIVITY – GUIDELINE	
	APPROXIMATE TIMING
Exercise Overview ▶ Review exercise plan ▶ Exercise Slides 1 – 3 (fire narrative)	12:30 PM – 12:45 PM
Initial Assessment Team (IAT) – Slide 4 ▶ Ask IAT members to assemble in the front of the room and to use their assessment tool/criteria to review the incident. ▶ Pose the question – "Will you activate?" Yes/no. ▶ If yes, review initial plan activation checklists.	12:45 PM – 1:00 PM
Conduct an IAP meeting – Slide 5	1:00 PM – 1:20 PM
▶ Teams "huddle" in groups to discuss their assigned objectives and look at plan for guidance.	1:20 PM – 1:50 PM
▶ Teams report out what they would be doing to meet their objectives. Note areas of duplication or areas not addressed.	1:50 PM – 2:20 PM
Debrief – Slide 6 ▶ What worked? ▶ What needs improvement	2:20 PM – 2:55 PM
Next steps	2:55 PM – 3:00 PM

Summary

This simple exercise is a powerful tool to orient teams and plans to each other. They are easy to develop and can provide great training at very little cost.

CHAPTER 13

How to conduct a tabletop exercise

Basic Tabletop Exercises are, by far, the most commonly held exercise. A Tabletop – even a Basic Tabletop – is a bit more realistic than an Orientation Exercise and is highly malleable. It can also be "spiced up" a bit by turning it into the Advanced Tabletop version (which has the Simulation Team present in the room). There are several different ways to construct and deliver a tabletop – it all goes back to your favorite question, *Why are we doing this exercise?*

- ▶ Basic Tabletop:
    - ▷ Basic narrative.
    - ▷ Several injects.
    - ▷ Discussion-based.
- ▶ Advanced Tabletop:
    - ▷ More detailed narrative.
    - ▷ More injects (delivered on Message Center form for a bit more realism).
    - ▷ Simulation Team in the room, acting as "outside world."

Tabletop exercise checklist

This checklist can be used as a guide and timeline for developing a Tabletop Exercises.

TABLETOP EXERCISE CHECKLIST		
ACTIVITY	**DATE**	**ASSIGNED TO**
12 weeks before		
☐ Select date and time for exercise.		
☐ Reserve room.		

TABLETOP EXERCISE CHECKLIST

ACTIVITY	DATE	ASSIGNED TO
☐ Send out a *"save the date"* communication (email, voicemail, fax, etc.) to the players.		
☐ Explore the question, *Why are we doing this exercise?* (See Chapter 4.)		
☐ Develop list of likely Exercise Design Team (EDT) Members. > Advanced TT: Ask Exercise Design Team members (3 to 5 people) to serve as Simulators on the day of the exercise.		
11 weeks before		
☐ Develop the goal and objectives of the exercise.		
☐ Validate goal and objectives with appropriate individuals; modify accordingly.		
☐ Develop exercise narrative.		
☐ Develop complete *exercise plan*.		
☐ Develop Document Summary form.		
☐ Select dates for three Design Team meetings		
☐ Send out *email invite to EDT members*.		
9 weeks before		
☐ Design Team meeting #1: Validate exercise plan. Discuss exercise injects. Issue homework assignment for injects (due in 7 days).		
8 weeks before		
☐ Review homework, tweak, revise, and send back full inject list along with any revisions to the Exercise Plan to the team.		
7 weeks before		
☐ Design Team meeting #2. Review all injects. Evaluate status. Need more homework? Need meeting #3? Make those decisions; if necessary, issue homework assignment #2.		
6 weeks before		
☐ Review homework, tweak, revise and send back full inject list, along with any revisions to the Exercise Plan to the team.		
☐ Write *radio broadcast*.		
5 weeks before		

TABLETOP EXERCISE CHECKLIST

ACTIVITY	DATE	ASSIGNED TO
☐ Design Team meeting #3. Review all injects and finalize. ☐ Record radio broadcast.		
4 weeks before		
☐ Send *exercise agenda* to players. Include goal, objectives, and agenda/timeline.		
☐ Insert exercise injects into a slide deck.		
☐ Develop participant evaluation.		
Two weeks before		
☐ Order catering for exercise (coffee, lunch, etc.). If ordering lunch, try to get a box lunch; this makes the food serving go much faster.		
☐ Determine how to play the radio broadcast. Do any necessary troubleshooting.		
Three weeks before		
☐ Order audio-visual equipment (LCD projector, flip charts, etc).		
One week before		
☐ Order printed materials (Exercise plan, Evaluations, other documents as necessary).		
☐ Send follow-up email to players reminding them of the exercise. Include reminder of any items they may need to bring.		
☐ Advanced TT: Orient Simulators (your Design Team volunteers or others) on how to be a Simulator. Review likely responses and role play.		
Day before exercise		
☐ Set up room.		
☐ Verify proper functioning of all audio-visual equipment.		
☐ Play radio broadcast to ensure it plays with no issues.		
☐ Set up "parking lots." These are flip charts or whiteboard that will be used to capture any questions or issues that come up during the training but can't be addressed at that time.		
Exercise day		
☐ Conduct exercise.		

TABLETOP EXERCISE CHECKLIST		
ACTIVITY	DATE	ASSIGNED TO
☐ Collect participant evaluations at the end.		
☐ Collect and save and/or properly destroy exercise materials after the exercise.		
No longer than two weeks AFTER exercise		
☐ Write After-Action Report (AAR).		
No longer than three weeks AFTER exercise		
☐ Distribute AAR.		

▶ *Italicized sections are included as samples in the next section. Documents not included here can be found in Chapter 9, "Additional Documents."*

Basic tabletop exercise – sample materials

The following sample exercise materials are written for an Incident Management Team (IMT). It could easily be adapted for individual business units. If that's your goal, be sure to re-focus all of the materials towards a business unit and its specific issues and problems. (In the example below, the materials are focused on issues that have impact across the enterprise.)

"Save the date" communication

Please save the date for our bi-annual tabletop exercise to be held on <<date and time>> at <<company name>>. This tabletop exercise is critically important to ensure that our plans remain up-to-date, we are all familiar with them, and can execute quickly and efficiently if necessary. You will be playing an important role in the system and your attendance at this important event is critical. Please mark your calendar for <<date and time>>. The session will be held at the <<meeting location>>. Additional information will be sent a few weeks prior to the session. Thanks again – I look forward to seeing you on <<date>>

Don't forget to ask all players to send an RSVP back to you. Silence does not always equal affirmation. If you get no response, follow up.

Document summary

For a Tabletop Exercise, the most likely documents you will need are: Exercise Plan, exercise injects in document form, exercise injects on Message Center forms, participant evaluation, evaluator form. Other document summary formats can be found in Chapter 9.

TABLETOP EXERCISE DOCUMENT SUMMARY				
ITEMS NEEDED	PRINTING INSTRUCTIONS	DEVELOPMENT STATUS	WHO RECEIVES IT	DATE COMPLETED
Exercise Plan	B/W		Everyone	
All Exercise injects	B/W		Facilitator, Sim Team and Evaluator	
Injects on message center forms	B/W		One copy to facilitator	
Evaluator Form	B/W		Evaluators	
Participant evaluation	B/W		Everyone	

Agenda

Exercise Agenda <<date>>

Goals
- ▶ Recognize the importance of the planning process and planning effort.
- ▶ Experience an event that will impact the <<company name>> corporate headquarters.
- ▶ Assess the team's current level of readiness.

Objectives
- ▶ Practice and refine Incident Management Team (IMT) roles and processes.
- ▶ Increase comfort levels of IMT members with the roles and responsibilities.
- ▶ Improve teamwork and communications, within and across teams.

▶ Assess current status of plans: determine if there are holes or overlaps in plans and assess adequacy of plans.

Agenda

EXERCISE AGENDA		
ACTIVITY	TIME	DISCUSSION LEADER
Welcome and Introductions	9:00 AM – 9:30 AM	J. Smith
Tabletop exercise	9:30 AM – 11:45 PM	R. Facilitator
Working lunch Debrief	11:45 AM – 12:50 PM	R. Facilitator
Next steps	12:50 PM – 1:00 PM	J. Smith

Exercise Plan

ICS Workshop and Orientation Exercise <<date>>

1. Exercise type and scope
▶ Basic tabletop exercise.
▶ <<note who is playing>> is playing, all other departments and groups are simulated.

2. Goals
▶ Recognize the importance of the planning process and planning effort.
▶ Experience an event that will impact the <<company name>> corporate headquarters.
▶ Assess the team's current level of readiness.

3. Objectives

▶ Practice and refine Incident Management Team (IMT) roles and processes.

▶ Increase comfort levels of IMT members with the roles and responsibilities.

▶ Improve teamwork and communications, within and across teams.

▶ Assess current status of plans: determine if there are holes or overlaps in plans and assess adequacy of plans.

4. Agenda

EXERCISE AGENDA		
ACTIVITY	TIME	DISCUSSION LEADER
Welcome and introductions	9:00 AM – 9:30 AM	J. Smith
Tabletop exercise	9:30 AM – 11:45 PM	R. Facilitator
Working lunch debrief	11:45 AM – 12:50 PM	R. Facilitator
Next steps	12:50 PM – 1:00 PM	J. Smith

5. Instructions to participants

▶ Exercises have the greatest value if they are treated as real. Stay in role the entire time.

▶ This exercise will stay in "real-time." The timeframe within the exercise period will not accelerate. Once we begin, the clock simply ticks on.

▶ Don't just think about responding to what is coming at you – remember to keep one eye into the future and play the game of "what-if."

▶ As the exercise progresses, details may not be as complete as you would like. The value is in the process, the dialogue, and the experience. The design team has worked to make the situations as realistic as possible.

▶ You may only use what is in place as of today; if new equipment is being added next month, it is not in place and can't be used.

▶ Exercises are for learning; we expect mistakes. The goal is to develop the team and learn from the experience.

▶ In order to make this exercise work and to facilitate the learning process, a certain amount of "exercise magic" has been used. We ask you not to debate that something has happened, could have happened, or is available – it just is!

▶ There is no "pass" or "fail" in this exercise. It is expected that many mistakes will be made – an exercise is a valuable learning experience to see if the plans that   were developed are sufficient.

▶ There will be some observers visiting the exercise. They are there as "silent observers" to view the activities. There is to be no interaction between the observers and the exercise participants.

▶ Questions regarding the exercise should be directed to the exercise facilitator.

6. Communications

▶ All information in the narrative and that provided by the facilitator is to be considered valid. However, just like in a real disaster, messages can be jumbled, and rumors can start on incorrect information or assumptions. Multiple versions of the same problem may occur.

▶ If you need information from someone at another business unit table, get up and go speak to them. If you need information from someone who is not in the room, call them directly.

7. Exercise injects

▶ Periodic pre-scripted injects (messages) will be used throughout this exercise. The exercise facilitator will monitor the exercise and adjust the flow of messages to provide the maximum training benefit for the participants.

8. Evaluation

▶ The exercise will be evaluated by use of participant written evaluations, the debrief session, and evaluators' observations based on the objectives.

9. General exercise assumptions

▶ All information in the narrative is to be considered valid.

▶ All information provided by the facilitators is to be considered valid.

▶ Don't assume anything else. All information can be verified by asking the facilitator.

10. Specific exercise artificialities and assumptions

▶ Artificialities

▷ For the past two weeks, many employees at the corporate headquarters have been complaining of health ailments such as upper respiratory, flu-like symptoms including runny nose, itchy red eyes, scratchy throat, laryngitis and fatigue.

▷ The company has hired an industrial hygiene company to conduct an environmental survey of the building.

▷ The team is meeting <<note where you would be meeting since your facility is off limits.>>

▶ Assumptions

▷ Although plans and processes are not completely refined, this exercise is designed to execute the procedures in their current state of readiness.

11. Narrative

For the past two weeks many employees have been complaining of health ailments such as upper respiratory, flu-like symptoms including runny nose, itchy red eyes, scratchy throat, laryngitis and fatigue. The company has hired an industrial hygiene company to conduct an environmental survey of the building. The consulting firm is working closely with OSHA and the County Department of Public Health. The survey began two days ago.

Approximately 45 minutes ago, <<company name>> was notified by the County Department of Public Health that the office tower was to be evacuated immediately. No reason was given for the evacuation. It is unknown when the building can be re-occupied. The evacuation was orderly with the building rapidly emptying in 15 minutes. Employees left the building quickly leaving behind personal items such as coats, purses, keys and laptop computers expecting the time out of the facility to be of a short duration.

Your employees are out on the sidewalk across the street. Employees are milling around, not sure what to do next. Some have also heard "rumors" of hazardous materials such as anthrax or other biological weapons and are quite anxious. They are awaiting information from the management team. Many emergency responders have surrounded the buildings. There are numerous Hazardous Materials teams and responders dressed in full Level One "space suits." Police are keeping people back from the buildings.

Your team has assembled to assess the situation. You have no idea how long you will be out of the building nor do you know the cause of the evacuation. You have heard rumors of some toxic material in the building and the potential for an outage of days to weeks. You have issued no statements or any communication directives to employees at this time. You are awaiting word from the Department of Public Health as to the length of the outage.

Exercise injects

Here is a sampling of injects for a Basic Tabletop exercise. Once the content was reviewed and agreed to by the Design Team, they would be cut-and-pasted into a slide deck. They could also be pasted into Message Center forms.

BASIC TABLETOP EXERCISE INJECTS			
#	TIME	CALLER	INJECT CONTENT
1			Radio Broadcast (play after reviewing exercise plan)
2			The County Department of Public Health notifies the Company that the substance found in the building is a mold called Stachybotrys Chartarum. It has been discharging mycotoxins in the building for the past few weeks. It is highly dangerous. The building is completely off limits. It will be at least three days before you can enter the building. It may be longer.

BASIC TABLETOP EXERCISE INJECTS

#	TIME	CALLER	INJECT CONTENT
3			The local ABC and NBC affiliates are calling for an interview. Both of the stations are planning special news report that will air on the evening news (approximately three hours from now). They would like an executive to do an on camera interview and want an official statement from the Company. If they don't hear back from you they will note that the Company has "no comment" in their broadcast.
4			Due to the suspected contamination of the building, the Department of Public Health has made the decision to not let cars out of the garage until it can be tested. This will be at least 24 – 48 hours. Employees are quite upset; many have no way home easily. Others have personal items in their cars they cannot access. What are your plans?
5			Many employees are frantic as they have their house and car keys in the building and can't get home. Many left their wallets and other critical documents in their purses or briefcases. What can you do to get them their personal possessions?
6			Human Resources have referred two supervisors (Sales and IT) who are concerned about several employees in their departments. Their families have called them to express their anxiety regarding the sick building and their own personal illness and that of the employee. They want to know what The Company is doing to take care of them. "After all this is now a workers comp case and it is a case of poor maintenance!"
7			Employees are asking about when they should return to work. What are you going to tell them? How can you keep staff informed of the company status on an on-going basis, there is nothing set up in advance for this purpose?
8			Hourly and salaried employees want to know what the rules are regarding compensation. How long will the Company pay them without requiring them to go into their vacation time?
9			What do you tell sales force in the field regarding this situation? How do you communicate with them? What should they be telling customers who can't reach the call center or the corporate headquarters?
10			Accounting wants to know how they are going to get their critical mail delivered over the next few days. They are expecting several large checks from major creditors.

Radio broadcast

This is <<broadcaster name>> with <<Radio Station>>, reporting from the <<company name and location>>, where the County Department of Public Health has just condemned the company's buildings due to a significant infection of the deadly mold Stachybotrys chartarum.

It all started a number of weeks ago, when many employees in the <<company name>> became ill with various complaints, ranging from such minor problems as runny noses, itchy red eyes, and scratchy throats, to more serious problems like laryngitis, upper respiratory problems, and unexplained fatigue. The medical problems came to a head yesterday when two employees were sent to <<local hospital>>, one with pulmonary edema and one hemorrhaging. We have been unable to confirm their condition, but we are led to believe they are both in serious condition.

After the employees were hospitalized, <<company name>> hired an industrial hygiene company to conduct an environmental survey of the building. This firm has confirmed it worked closely with the OSHA and the County Department of Public Health (DPH) to determine the likely cause of the employees' medical problems. After yesterday's initial inspection, it was discovered that the buildings have become a breeding ground for Stachybotrys chartarum.

This is a tenacious strain, as individuals with chronic exposure to the toxin produced by this fungus can experience such health issues as cold and flu symptoms, memory loss, muscle aches, sore throats, diarrhea, headaches, fatigue, dermatitis, intermittent local hair loss, cancer, and generalized malaise. At its worst, the toxins produced by this fungus can suppress and eventually destroy the immune system, affecting lymphoid tissue and bone marrow. Given the right conditions, Stachybotrys is capable of creating multiple toxic chemicals in its spores, as well as in the tiny fragments that can become airborne.

Thanks to the modern convenience of our HVAC systems,

these spores and fragments can then be spread throughout a building quickly. Even dead spores are still allergenic and toxigenic, and if they are disturbed, they can set off many mycotoxins that can be even more toxic than the original. Apparently, that's what happened at <<company name>>.

This is <<broadcaster name>> with <<Radio Station>>, reporting live on the deadly mold situation infecting the <<company name>>. Back to you in the studio.

Participant evaluation

	Please circle one				
	STRONGLY DISAGREE		**NEUTRAL**		**STRONGLY AGREE**
1. The scenario was realistic.	1	2	3	4	5
2. The exercise encouraged my participation.	1	2	3	4	5
3. The exercise met my expectations.	1	2	3	4	5
4. The facilitator was effective.	1	2	3	4	5
5. I understand my role in a situation like this.	1	2	3	4	5
6. Overall, what did you think of the exercise?					
7. What was the most helpful?					
8. What could we improve upon?					
9. What three things should this team focus on for the next exercise?					

Other participant evaluation samples can be found in Chapter 9.

Advanced tabletop exercise timing guideline – half day

The following is a guideline on how to conduct an Advanced Tabletop exercise using the materials included in this chapter. The agenda assumes the exercise runs from 9:00 AM to 1:00 PM.

ADVANCED TABLETOP EXERCISE TIMING GUIDELINE – HALF DAY

EXERCISE ACTIVITY – GUIDELINE	TIME

▶ Introductions (if necessary).
▶ Review exercise and how it will work.
▶ Introduce concept of the Simulation Team in the room.
   > If the players need to speak to anyone from the outside world, they call the Simulation Team who will "become" those people.
   > Explain purpose of Sim Team.
▶ Review exercise plan.
	9:00 AM – 9:25 AM

▶ Play radio broadcast	9:25 AM – 9:30 AM
▶ Players divide into their teams, develop their action plans and respond to the injects. > As teams discuss issues and reference their plans, injects will be delivered even as the other activities may be going on.	9:30 AM – 11:00 AM
▶ Group report outs > This time segment will depend on how many groups need to report (figure 5 to 7 minutes per group).	11:00 AM – 11:45 AM

Lunch and debrief:
▶ Ask players to grab lunch and get seated (a box lunch will help this go a bit faster).
▶ Debrief:
   > What worked?
   > What needs improvement
	11:45 AM – 12:50 PM

Next steps	12:50 PM – 1:00 PM

Advanced tabletop exercise timing guideline – full day

The following is a guideline on how to conduct an advanced tabletop exercise using the materials included in this chapter. For this exercise, there are two narratives; the second narrative moves the exercise clock forward. This agenda assumes the exercise runs from 9:00 AM to 5:00 PM.

ADVANCED TABLETOP EXERCISE TIMING GUIDELINE – FULL DAY

EXERCISE ACTIVITY – GUIDELINE	TIME

▶ Introductions (if necessary).
▶ Review exercise and how it will work.
▶ Introduce concept of the Simulation Team in the room.
  > If the players need to speak to anyone from the outside world, they call the Simulation Team who will "become" those people.
  > Explain purpose of Sim Team.
▶ Review exercise plan.
	9:00 AM – 9:25 AM

▶ Play radio broadcast	9:25 AM – 9:30 AM

▶ Exercise One:
  > Players divide into their teams, develop their action plans and respond to the injects.
  > As teams discuss issues and reference their plans, injects will be delivered even as the other activities may be going on.
	9:30 AM – 11:15 AM

▶ Develop team reports for management briefing	11:15 AM – 11:45 AM
▶ Conduct Executive management briefing of Exercise One (Executive management can be real Executives or simulated).	11:45 AM – 12:00 PM

Lunch and Exercise One debrief:
▶ Ask players to grab lunch and get seated (a box lunch will help this go a bit faster).
▶ Debrief:
  > What worked?
  > What needs improvement?
  > What do I want to do differently in the afternoon?
	12:00 PM – 12:45 PM

▶ Exercise Two:
  > Move the clock forward.
  > Review new exercise plan.
  > Begin delivering Exercise Two injects.
  > Continue with same format as Exercise One.
	12:45 PM – 3:15 PM

▶ Develop team reports for management briefing	3:15 PM – 3:45 PM

ADVANCED TABLETOP EXERCISE TIMING GUIDELINE – FULL DAY	
EXERCISE ACTIVITY – GUIDELINE	**TIME**
► Conduct Executive management briefing of Exercise Two (Executive management can be real Executives or simulated).	3:45 PM – 4:00 PM
Exercise Two debrief: ► Allow players a brief break, then be seated. ► Debrief: 　> What worked? 　> What needs improvement 　> How did things go differently in the afternoon?	4:00 PM – 4:50 PM
Next steps	4:50 PM – 5:00 PM

Summary

The highly flexible Tabletop exercise can be modified many different ways to achieve the results you are looking for. Teams can do this style of exercise several times before moving on to a more advanced style. If time is limited and/or resources are short, you can, of course, keep your teams in this style of exercise, challenging them by "mixing up" the narratives, using an in-room Simulation Team, and using more and different audio-visual tools.

CHAPTER 14

Creating reality:
How to conduct a functional exercise

One step beyond

Functional exercises are fully simulated events. They are often described by the players as being very realistic. "My hands were sweating and my heart was pounding; I thought the incident had really happened," is not a surprising participant comment. Participants actually perform all of the activities that they are expected to during an event (within the confines of the exercise environment) and all exercise injects (see Chapter 6) are delivered by a Simulation Team member or an audio-visual tool. In a Functional exercise, however, there is no field response or the movement of resources in the field. So the team would order a resource, but wouldn't actually deploy them. This exercise has a variety of bells and whistles that makes it quite different from a Tabletop.

Bell and whistle #1: Simulation Team

This type of exercise is very interactive. The Simulation Team is the main driver in a Functional exercise. They are located in another room (yet – hopefully – close to the exercise) and deliver most of the injects by phone. A comprehensive Simulation Team orientation is critical to ensure the Sim Team members are fully prepared to respond and interact with the players in a more robust fashion than simply handing out forms or only making outbound calls.

Bell and whistle #2: Phone directory

You will need to create a phone directory in order to provide the exercise players with their list of "outside world" phone numbers – numbers that the Simulation Team will be answering. I begin creating the directory by thinking about who in the outside world the exercise players would likely need to contact. I then build those names, entities, or companies into the directory. And because I can't think of everyone they might want to call, I will normally list several "Genius-of-all-trades" entries who can impersonate anyone not otherwise listed in the directory[10].

During the exercise briefing (once everyone has gathered before the exercise playtime), I will review the use of the phone directory and how the Simulation Team works. I have found that this helps avoid much of their potential confusion. Be sure to allocate time in your remarks to cover these critical exercise issues.

Bell and whistle #3: Controllers/Evaluators

You will very likely have one or both of these roles in attendance during a Functional exercise. And, as expected, the larger the exercise, the more Controllers/Evaluators you will likely have. Controllers may be used to assist the Simulation Team in delivering some injects, but more than likely they will track the delivery of injects and note the teams' performance.

Bell and whistle #4: Executives

A Functional exercise is a great exercise for engaging your executives. When I conduct these exercises with an Incident Management Team (IMT), I like to conclude the exercise with an executive briefing to the real executives. This provides the Incident Commander (IC) with valuable practice facing a real executive and the questions a real executive might likely ask. An Executive Briefing can be done face-to-face or by a conference bridge.

To determine which one is best for you to do, I recommend that you do in the exercise what you would do in real life. (People fall back to their level of training, so only train and exercise what you want them to do during a real situation.) So, if your plan states that the executives would be briefed in person, then you should have them show up in person for their exercise briefing. (In this case, don't forget to get the exercise date and time on their calendars well in advance!)

---

10 I used to call this role "Jack-" or "Jill-of-all-Trades. However, as a Mac user since 1984, in recent years, I changed it to "Genius-of-all-Trades," in deference to Apple and their "Geniuses," brilliant folks who can answer any tech problem.

Prepping the executives for the exercise

First, you will need to develop an Executive Briefing or summary document. This document would include the basic information that they need to know, such as the briefing time, the call-in number and passcode (if it's being held by conference call), and your expectations for their performance. This document should also include the highlights of the narrative and artificialities. Ideally, this briefing document should be no more than two pages.

With all the "trench-coat secrecy" around your exercise, why send them the information in advance? Well, since they have not been part of the exercise, they are being dropped in at the end of an intensive activity being done by other people. They haven't been part of the action prior to walking into the room or dialing into the call. They need to have an idea about what has happened so that they can be "in role" and ask pertinent questions. Don't forget – the Executive Briefing is not really an exercise to test **their** abilities, it's to test the IC's ability to provide executive-appropriate information. You could think of them as acting like an executive Simulation Team – although, of course, they are the real thing! Yes, the executives are learning how it "should work" in an emergency, and where and how they will receive their information, but they are primarily providing a real-time experience for the exercise players.

If possible, I like to have a face-to-face meeting with the chosen executive(s) before the exercise to give them a briefing. This short session (usually 30 minutes or less) gives me the opportunity to set expectations and to review the key aspects of the exercise. If their schedule does not allow for such a meeting, then I will send the Executive Briefing document to them – and their administrative assistant – 24 hours before the exercise. In the cover email, I ask them not to forward or share the document with any of their direct reports to avoid having a "leak" the day before the exercise.

During the exercise, there are a couple of options available to conduct the briefing. You could do it in front of the entire team via a speakerphone. This allows everyone to listen in. You could also hold it in another room for more privacy. The politics of your organization will usually be the driving factor here. If the topics to be discussed are not too sensitive or confidential, having all team members hear the actual briefing and the type of questions the executives ask can be a great learning experience for all team members.

Bell and whistle #5: Press conference

Do you have communications objectives in your exercise plan? Does your communications group desire to be further stretched in the exercise? If so, having a 'press conference' is a great way to deepen their experience, and to more fully exercise their plan and the individuals who drive it. Your Simulation Team – Oscar®-quality actors all by now – can become 'reporters' to conduct a press conference.

So without real paparazzi and reporters, where do you get the questions? You have a couple of options for this, too. The easiest thing to do is to develop them yourself. This is a good choice if I want to be sure that the questions have a certain tone – or perhaps I want to really control what is being asked. Another option is to ask the Simulation Team to design them. If you choose this method, you can simply ask each Sim Team member to jot down at least two likely press questions as the exercise progresses. (Hint: If you don't create the press questions yourself, I recommend reviewing the Sim Team submissions before the press conference to make sure they aren't "off-the-wall" or too abrasive.)

To carry out the press conference, you guessed it – you have options. Like the Executive Briefing, you could conduct it in front of the exercise room so all can hear it, or you can do it in another room for more privacy. To make it more realistic, you should arrange for some sort of podium for the communications person to stand behind when they read their statement. The Simulation Team (a.k.a., your "reporters") would be seated in front of the room to ask their questions.

You might also consider videotaping the session so the communications person is able to see their own performance, both when they read their statement, and when they answer "reporter" questions. Another plus of having cameras in the room – it instills a bit more reality.

Functional exercise words of wisdom

Functional exercises are more time-intensive and more expensive to prepare than Orientation and Tabletop exercises. In exchange, however, they provide incredible value to the participants both in deepening their knowledge and broadening their experience. Be sure to allocate sufficient time to adequately develop and plan the exercise. As a guideline, for your first Functional exercise, begin the planning at least four months in advance. As you become more proficient in exercise design, you might be able to shorten the design and prep time. This is a highly visible exercise and will likely attract a lot of attention in the company. You will want to make sure you have crossed all the t's and dotted all the i's – and that takes time and preparation.

Functional exercise checklist

This checklist can be used as a four-month timeline and guide for developing a Functional exercise.

FUNCTIONAL EXERCISE CHECKLIST		
ACTIVITY	**DATE**	**ASSIGNED TO**
16 weeks before		
☐ Select date and time for exercise.		
☐ Reserve exercise and Simulation Team rooms (and any other rooms as necessary).		
☐ Send out a "save the date" communication (email, voicemail, fax, etc.) to the players.		
☐ Explore the question, Why are we doing this exercise? (See Chapter 4.)		
☐ Develop list of likely Exercise Design Team (EDT) Members. > Ask all Exercise Design Team members to serve as Simulators on the day of the exercise.		
☐ Confirm whether executives will participate in the exercise. Send a "save the date" email to executive assistants.		
☐ Confirm whether communications team will conduct a press conference.		
14 weeks before		
☐ Develop the goal and objectives of the exercise.		
☐ Validate goal and objectives with appropriate individuals; modify accordingly.		

- ☐ Develop exercise narrative.
- ☐ Develop complete exercise plan.
- ☐ Develop Document Summary form.
- ☐ Select dates for four Design Team meetings.
- ☐ Send out email invite to EDT members.

12 weeks before

- ☐ Design Team meeting #1: Validate exercise plan. Discuss exercise injects. Issue homework assignment for injects (due in 7 days).

10 weeks before

- ☐ Review homework, tweak, revise, and send back full inject list along with any revisions to the Exercise Plan to the team.

9 weeks before

- ☐ Design Team meeting #2. Review all injects. Evaluate status. Issue homework assignment #2 (due in 7 days).

8 weeks before

- ☐ Review homework, tweak, revise and send back full inject list, along with any revisions to the Exercise Plan to the team.

7 weeks before

- ☐ Design Team meeting #3. Review all injects. Evaluate status. Issue homework assignment #3 (due in 7 days).

6 weeks before

- ☐ Review homework, tweak, revise and send back full inject list, along with any revisions to the Exercise Plan to the team.
- ☐ Write radio broadcast(s)

5 weeks before

- ☐ Design Team meeting #4. Review all injects and finalize. Evaluate status. Need more homework? Need more meetings? Make those decisions; if necessary, issue more homework, set up more meetings.
- ☐ Record radio broadcast(s).

4 weeks before

- ☐ Send exercise agenda to players. Include goal, objectives, and agenda/timeline.

- ☐ Develop Simulation Team evaluation.
- ☐ Develop participant evaluation.
- ☐ Develop controller/evaluator/observer form.
- ☐ Develop phone directory 'shell' (entries with no phone numbers).

Two weeks before

- ☐ Order catering for exercise (coffee, lunch, etc.). If ordering lunch, try to get a box lunch; this makes the food serving go much faster.
- ☐ Determine how to play the radio broadcast. Do any necessary troubleshooting.

Three weeks before

- ☐ Order audio-visual equipment (LCD projector, flip charts, etc).

Two weeks before

- ☐ Prepare Executive Briefing document.
- ☐ Confirm which of your Design Team will be your Simulators. If you have too many, some can become observers; if you have too few, start lining up others.

One week before

- ☐ Order printed materials (Exercise plan, Evaluations, other documents as necessary).
- ☐ Send follow-up email to players reminding them of the exercise. Include reminder of any items they may need to bring.
- ☐ Orient Simulators on how to be a Simulator. Review likely responses and role play.
- ☐ Orient Evaluators/Controllers/Observers.

Two days before exercise

- ☐ Add phone numbers to the phone directory.

Day before exercise

- ☐ Set up room.
- ☐ Check phone lines.
- ☐ Verify proper functioning of all audio-visual equipment.
- ☐ Play radio broadcast to ensure it plays with no issues.
- ☐ Determine which room will be used for the press conference; if separate room than the exercise, set up.

☐ Set up Simulation Team room and check phones.		
☐ Set up "parking lots." (Flip charts or whiteboard used to capture any questions or issues that come up during the exercise but can't be addressed at that time.)		
☐ Conduct 30-minute exercise briefing for the executives. (If unable to do in person, then send executive briefing via email.)		
Exercise day		
☐ Conduct exercise.		
☐ Collect participant evaluations at the end.		
☐ Collect and properly destroy exercise materials after the exercise.		
No longer than two weeks AFTER exercise		
☐ Write After-Action Report (AAR).		
No longer than three weeks AFTER exercise		
☐ Distribute AAR.		

▶ Italicized documents are included as samples in the next section. Documents not included here can be found in Chapter 9, "Additional Documents."

Basic functional exercise – sample materials

The following sample exercise materials are written for an Incident Management Team (IMT). It could easily be adapted for individual business units. If that's your goal, be sure to refocus all of the materials towards a business unit and its specific issues and problems. (In the example below, the materials are focused on issues that have impact across the enterprise.)

"Save the date" communication

Please save the date for our bi-annual Functional exercise to be held on <<date and time>> at <<company name>>. This Functional exercise is critically important to ensure that our plans remain up-to-date, we are all familiar with them, and can execute them quickly and efficiently if necessary. You will be playing an important role in the system and your attendance at this important event is critical. Please mark your calendar for <<date and time>>. The session will be held at the <<meeting location>>. Additional information will be sent a few weeks prior to the session. Thanks again – I look forward to seeing you on <<date>>

Don't forget to ask all players to send an RSVP back to you. Silence does not always equal affirmation. If you get no response, follow up.

Document summary

For a Functional Exercise, you will likely need more documents than for a Tabletop Exercise. Other document summary formats can be found in Chapter 9.

ITEMS NEEDED	PRINTING INSTRUCTIONS	DEVELOPMENT STATUS	WHO RECEIVES IT	DATE COMPLETED
Exercise Plan	B/W		Everyone	
All Exercise injects	B/W		Facilitator, Sim Team &Evaluator	
Phone Directory	Print on colored paper		Everyone	
Evaluator Form	B/W		Evaluators	
Sim Team Evaluation	B/W		Sim Team	
Participant Evaluation	B/W		Everyone	
Executive Briefing	Sent as a PDF to the executives 24 hours in advance of exercise		Executives	

FUNCTIONAL EXERCISE DOCUMENT SUMMARY

Agenda
Basic Functional Exercise Agenda <<date>>

Goal

Assess ability of the <<name of team>> to manage a major regional event and continue to expand field response and communication activities.

Objectives

▶ Assess the ability of the communications team to develop the <<company name>> message, and produce the following communication materials: student, parent and employee communications via the emergency notification system (ENS), press releases, and community notifications.

▶ Assess the effectiveness of the ENS and its use during the exercise.

▶ Assess the ability of the Incident Commander to brief Executive Leadership Team.

▶ Assess the ability of the Incident Commander (IC), and designated Team Leaders to conduct a timely Incident Action Planning meeting and develop a written IAP.

▶ Incorporate the Satellite Operations Centers (SOC) into the exercise, and assess communications between the SOCs and the EOC. Determine gaps or overlaps, and note areas for improvement.

Agenda

FUNCTIONAL EXERCISE AGENDA		
ACTIVITY	TIME	DISCUSSION LEADER
Welcome and Introductions Review exercise plan	8:00 AM – 8:30 AM	J. Smith
Functional Exercise	8:30 AM – 11:45 PM	R. Facilitator
Executive Briefing	11:45 AM – 12:10 PM	Incident Commander
Press Conference	12:10 PM – 12:30 PM	Communications Team
Working Lunch Debrief	12:30 PM – 1:20 PM	R. Facilitator
Next steps	1:20 PM – 1:30 PM	J. Smith

Exercise plan
Basic Functional Exercise <<date>>

1. Exercise type and scope

▶ This is a Functional exercise, using the statewide "Shake Out" exercise narrative, pre-scripted messages, media inputs, and a Simulation Team.

▶ <<note who is playing>> is playing, all other departments and groups are simulated.

2. Goal

Assess ability of the <<name of team>> to manage a major regional event and continue to expand field response and communication activities.

3. Objectives

▶ Assess the ability of the communications team to develop the <<company name>> message, and produce the following communication materials: student, parent and employee communications via the emergency notification system (ENS), press releases, and community notifications.

▶ Assess the effectiveness of the ENS and its use during the exercise.

▶ Assess the ability of the Incident Commander to brief Executive Leadership Team.

▶ Assess the ability of the Incident Commander (IC), and designated Team Leaders to conduct a timely Incident Action Planning meeting and develop a written IAP.

▶ Incorporate the Satellite Operations Centers (SOC) into the exercise, and assess communications between the SOCs and the EOC. Determine gaps or overlaps, and note areas for improvement.

4. Agenda

FUNCTIONAL EXERCISE AGENDA		
ACTIVITY	**TIME**	**DISCUSSION LEADER**
Welcome and Introductions Review exercise plan	8:00 AM – 8:30 AM	J. Smith
Functional Exercise	8:30 – 11:45 PM	R. Facilitator
Executive Briefing	11:45 – 12:10 PM	Incident Commander
Press Conference	12:10 – 12:30 PM	Communications Team
Working Lunch Debrief	12:30 – 1:20 PM	R. Facilitator
Next steps	1:20 – 1:30 PM	J. Smith

5. Instructions to participants

▶ Exercises have the greatest value if they are treated as real. Stay in role the entire time.

▶ This exercise will stay in "real-time." The timeframe within the exercise period will not accelerate. Once we begin, the clock simply ticks on.

▶ Don't just think about responding to what is coming at you – remember to keep one eye into the future and play the game of "what-if."

▶ As the exercise progresses, details may not be as complete as you would like. The value is in the process, the dialogue, and the experience. The design team has worked to make the situations as realistic as possible.

▶ You may only use what is in place as of today; if new equipment is being added next month, it is not in place and can't be used.

▶ Exercises are for learning; we expect mistakes. The goal is to develop the team and learn from the experience.

▶ In order to make this exercise work and to facilitate the learning process, a certain amount of "exercise magic" has been used. We ask you not to debate that something has happened, could have happened, or is available – it just is!

▶ There is no "pass" or "fail" in this exercise. It is expected that many mistakes will be made – an exercise is a valuable learning experience to see if the plans that were developed are sufficient.

▶ There will be some observers visiting the exercise. They are there as "silent observers" to view the activities. There is to be no interaction between the observers and the exercise participants.

▶ Questions regarding the exercise should be directed to the exercise facilitator.

6. *Communications*

▶ As part of what we call "exercise magic," phones, Internet, and fax machines will be working during the exercise. This is an artificiality of the exercise, but will allow us to move through the exercise with a bit more ease.

▶ The exercise participants will simulate all communications.

▶ A Simulation Team will act as the "outside world" for this exercise. Problems must be solved by calling the Simulation Team. This includes any call that you would make to find out information, order equipment, etc.

▶ You will likely receive calls and additional information throughout the exercise from numerous entities.

▶ All information in the narrative and provided by the facilitators and Simulation Team is to be considered valid. However, just like in a real disaster, messages can be jumbled and rumors started on incorrect information or assumptions. Multiple versions of the same problem may occur.

▶ There will be communications between the EOC, the Simulation Team, and all of the participating SOCs.

7. *Exercise injects*

▶ Periodic pre-scripted injects (messages) will be used throughout this exercise. The exercise facilitator will monitor the exercise and adjust the flow of messages to provide the maximum training benefit for the participants.

8. Evaluation

▶ The exercise will be evaluated by use of participant written evaluations, the debrief session, and evaluators' observations based on the objectives.

9. General exercise assumptions

▶ All information in the narrative is to be considered valid.

▶ All information provided by the facilitators is to be considered valid.

▶ Don't assume anything else. All information can be verified by asking the facilitator.

10. Specific exercise artificialities and assumptions

▶ Artificialities

▷ An earthquake occurred this morning, <<date and time>>. It took two minutes for the shaking to travel and be felt in <<city of exercise>>.

▷ The quake was a rupture of the San Andreas Fault at Bombay Beach, northeast of the Salton Sea.

▶ Assumptions

▷ It is sunny, with a light breeze. There are no Santa Ana winds today.

▷ The time is the real time.

11. Narrative

The earthquake that was felt in Pasadena this morning at 10:21 AM was a magnitude 7.8, and has created substantial damage from its epicenter at Bombay Beach. The ground on the two sides of the San Andreas fault is offset nearly 44 feet. [11]

As the earthquake's rupture front traveled up the fault, it sent out seismic waves that shook the ground, shifting emergency generators, overturning computers, cracking airport runways, and igniting fires. The Coachella Valley felt the shaking for almost a minute, the earthquake waves bouncing between

---

11   State of California, The Great Shakeout Narrative, Shakeout Resources http://www.shakeout.org/resources/index.html

the rock walls of the valley's edges.

As the Coachella Valley was in its last few seconds of shaking, some of the seismic waves finally reached the sediment of Los Angeles, which started to shake vigorously. Strong shaking continued throughout the entire Los Angeles area for 55 seconds, an eternity to those who remember the strong shaking during the 1994 Northridge earthquake – which lasted only 7 seconds.

12. Regional damage information

People

▶ The prolonged, strong shaking in Los Angeles has heavily damaged – and sometimes collapsed – hundreds of old brick buildings, hundreds of older commercial and industrial concrete buildings, many wood frame buildings, and even a few, fairly new high-rise steel buildings.

▶ The building damage caused tens of thousands of injuries and hundreds of deaths, and stranded many thousands of people without homes or jobs.

Transportation

▶ The I-15 Freeway has been severed.

▶ The rupture front dismantled the ten miles of Interstate 10 freeway that straddles the San Andreas Fault. The eastern part of Riverside County is now cut off from the western part.

▶ Electric trains have been immobilized.

▶ Other than I-15 and I-10, the State highway system has fared well. Seismic retrofit work has paid off, and the only highway deaths have been in crashes caused by intense earthquake shaking. However, the long duration of shaking has taken its toll on bridges and overpasses within local jurisdictions.

▶ Air traffic is being diverted from all southern California airports.

▶ Many surface streets are impassable. The Fire Department is unable to respond quickly to many calls because their equipment cannot easily maneuver through the damaged streets, debris, or abandoned cars.

Communication

▶ Phone systems are overwhelmed; there are no dial tones.

▶ Across the region, phone systems, including cellular and 911, are unusable, overwhelmed by the vast number of attempted calls.

Utilities

▶ Electrical service remains out throughout southern California.

▶ Pipelines have snapped and electrical transmission lines have failed.

▶ Natural gas is disrupted. There have already been gas leaks reported in all areas, many of which caused numerous fires due to downed power lines.

▶ Water and sewer pipes have cracked.

Schools, hospitals and care facilities

▶ No hospitals have seen complete collapses, but many hospital buildings are nonfunctional. Some hospital structures survived the shaking but must close due to nonstructural damage, such as water pipes that broke and flooded the facility.

Other

▶ Over 1,600 fires have been causing problems throughout the area. There are not enough emergency personnel to immediately respond to every call for help. Worse, response is slowed by roads that are impassable due to damage, building debris, or abandoned cars. Worse still, in many places the water system is damaged, leaving inadequate water pressure for fire-fighting efforts.

▶ Aftershocks are occurring, and are undoing some of the recovery efforts in progress, or diverting aid workers from other areas.

13. <<company>> status

People

▶ There are reports of injuries but there are no confirmations or numbers yet.

Utilities

▶ There are no utilities – no electricity, no water, no sewer, and no natural gas.

▷ There are reported gas leaks on campus.

▶ There is no phone service – cell or landline; even internal lines are overloaded. Some may be damaged.

Buildings

▶ There is significant building damage. You will learn specific building status throughout the exercise.

Mission-critical activities at risk

▶ Unknown at this time.

Communication

▶ No communications have been issued.

Exercise injects

Here is a sampling of injects for a Basic Functional exercise that would be cut-and-pasted into a slide deck. They could also be pasted into Message Center forms.

BASIC FUNCTIONAL EXERCISE INJECT SAMPLES					
#	TIME	SIM TEAM	ROUTE EOC/ SOC	CALLER	INJECT CONTENT
1					Radio Broadcast (play after reviewing exercise plan)
2				George Keck, Security Officer	The vehicles parked in the rear garage are trapped and unable to get out to the street because the rubble is blocking the driveway. The employees are frantic – what can we do to help them get their cars out? Anything?
3				Larry Taylor, Engineer	There is someone trapped in the elevator of the building and we can't get him out. What should we do?
4				Jane Williams, wife of Jack Williams, security guard	Oh, please help me! I heard there were deaths on campus and my husband hasn't come called me to check in. Can you tell me who the victims are?
5				Jackson Douglas, Chief Engineer	One of the four emergency generators started, restoring some power for lighting but the others are not responding. We are trying to determine the issue but it will take some time.

BASIC FUNCTIONAL EXERCISE INJECT SAMPLES

#	TIME	SIM TEAM	ROUTE EOC/ SOC	CALLER	INJECT CONTENT
6				Emily Cassidy, Call Center Manager	Before my staff leave, I want to know what I should be telling them. Are we getting paid for today? I assume the office will be closed tomorrow, too, but what about beyond that? Everyone is anxious and wants to get going...can you give me some guidance?
7				Ryan Adams, Cafeteria Mgr.	I'm reporting injuries over here. The kitchen equipment shifted during the earthquake spilled hot oil and liquids onto two staff. We were able to get them out of the building but they are in a lot of pain.
8				Sara Gwenn, National Sales Mgr.	Our website will be down for at least 24 hours and our HQ main phone numbers is not forwarding. We need to get a message out to our major clients. What options do we have?
9				David Green, Wall Street Journal	We are doing a story on the impact of the earthquake on the business community and what are there short-term strategies for recovery. We would like to interview a senior executive. Who could I speak to?
10				Abby Jana, R&D Director	Several of my staff has not used their computer ID tokens for over 30 days and they are not able to log in remotely. They need a new token and I can't reach anyone in the IT Help Desk. Can someone help me get new tokens for these mission critical staff?

Radio broadcast

This is <<personality>>, <<radio station>>,, reporting live from downtown Los Angeles, where this morning's earthquake has caused an incredible amount of damage here and for miles around.

The quake has left a path of destruction not unlike the great 1906 earthquake and fire in San Francisco. Here in downtown, there are at least 5 high-rise buildings that have collapsed, and authorities have red-tagged another ten. At this early point, the unofficial death toll is already at over 50, but authorities believe that number is very low, and is expected to rise to 250 over the next few hours and days. We have reports of injuries in the hundreds; this number, too, is expected to rise.

Hospitals, already struggling to take care of those patients who were already in their care, are seeing a dramatic increase in the number of citizens seeking medical attention. If you have a minor medical emergency, you are encouraged to stay home and take care of yourself for the time being to allow those with more serious injuries to receive the life-saving care that they need. It is expected that there will be close to 50,000 people requiring significant medical assistance in the coming days.

As for transportation issues, reports are still coming in from around the area, but the fault offset – the point where the ground shifted by more than 15 feet along the fault – has caused extensive damage to I-15 and I-10. In addition, shaking-related damage to highway bridges have rendered most freeways in Los Angeles, San Bernardino, and Riverside counties impassible at several locations, with authorities estimating that some damage will take as long as 5 to 7 months to repair. Authorities obviously suggest that if you don't need to be driving, don't. Stay home and tend to yourself and your neighbors.

On the personal side, it seemed like everyone who had a cell phone tried to call others to check on them and to let them know about themselves. Other battery-powered communication devices, like Blackberrys, laptops, and iPhones, were also turned on in a virtual tsunami of interpersonal communication attempts – attempts that, more often than not, failed. The messages that are the most reliable seem to be text messages, as they 'fly under the radar' of the cell phone system.

Although not felt very strongly here, there was a magnitude 7.0 aftershock about an hour ago. Like the first quake, it began near the Salton Sea; this one, however, ruptured to the south. Although this part of the state is a relatively unpopulated area, shaking was felt throughout Imperial and San Diego Counties, and into Mexico. Teams of firefighters from San Diego County had been getting ready to come to LA to offer mutual aid, but they have now diverted to respond to the damage in their own county. Authorities warn that significant aftershocks like this will also affect rescue efforts in progress.

This is <<personality>>, <<radio station>>, reporting live with continuing earthquake coverage. Back to you in the studio.

SIMULATION TEAM PHONE DIRECTORY

Exercise simulation team – they create the world for you!

1. When calling the Simulation Team, please remember:
2. The Genius-of-all-trades can be anyone you want them to be.
3. When calling the Sim Team they will answer the phone with "May I help you?"
   > Tell them who you are looking for!
4. If you need to find out "real information" (a fact) from a <<company name>> person or department, you may call them directly – tell them you are in an exercise (without the details) and need information to answer a question or resolve a problem.
5. The Simulation team has limited phones – if you call a number and get voice mail, don't leave a message. Just wait a few minutes and call back or try another Sim Team member. If it is busy, try again in a few minutes...just like real life.

State Office of Emergency Services	X1234		City Government, any department or person	X1234
Contractor, any	X2345		Police Department	X1234
Executive, any	X3456		Phone service – Cell, any vendor	X2345
Financial Institution, any	X4567			
Fire Department, any	X5678		Shipping vendors such as Fed Ex, USPS	X3456
Genius-of-all-trades	X6789			
Genius-of-all-trades	X7890		Software companies or products, any	X4567
Genius-of-all-trades	X1234			
Genius-of-all-trades	X2345		Structural Engineering firms, any	X5678
Genius-of-all-trades	X3456			
Genius-of-all-trades	X4567		Technology vendors, hardware, any	X6789
Hazardous Materials Team	X5678		Telecommunications hardware vendor, any	X7890
Hospital, any	X6789			
Hotels, any	X7890		Telephone: Local carrier	X1234
Insurance, any	X1234		Telephone: Long distance, MCI, ATT, Sprint	X2345
County Dept of Water and Power	X2345		Transportation vendors, i.e. buses, shuttles, cabs	X3456
County EOC	X3456			
County Health Dept.	X4567		US Dept of Homeland Security	X4567
Media, any electronic – TV, radio, Internet	X5678			
			USGS	X5678
Media, any print	X6789		Utilities, any others not mentioned in directory	X6789
Office supply vendor	X7890			

PARTICIPANT EVALUTION

Please circle one	STRONGLY DISAGREE		NEUTRAL		STRONGLY AGREE
1. The exercise design was realistic.	1	2	3	4	5
2. The scenario was a "real-world" (likely) event.	1	2	3	4	5
3. The exercise encouraged "my" participation.	1	2	3	4	5
4. The facilitator was effective.	1	2	3	4	5
5. The exercise met my expectations.	1	2	3	4	5
6. I feel prepared to respond at to a major earthquake at <<company>>.	1	2	3	4	5
7. My family and I are prepared at home for a major earthquake.	1	2	3	4	5

8. Overall, what did you think of the exercise?

9. What did you think was the most helpful?

10. What could we improve on?

11. What are the two most important things that <<company name>> should do to prepare for a major earthquake?

SIMULATION TEAM EXERCISE EVALUATION

Thank you for participating in this important exercise! In order for us to make these activities meaningful, your feedback is very important to us. Please take a few moments to comment on your experience.

1. Overall, what did you think of the exercise?

2. How was your experience as a Sim Team member? Please explain.

3. What did you think was the most helpful?

4. What could we improve on? How could we make the Sim Team experience better?

5. Is there anything in particular that you would like to see in future exercises?

EVALUATOR / OBSERVER FORM

OBSERVER NAME: TEAM OBSERVING:

Role of the Evaluator/Observer

The exercise design team has developed these objectives with a series of metrics for the exercise. The evaluators are to use the metrics to determine if the objectives have been met. We understand that this will be somewhat subjective by the evaluator and you can't be everywhere at once, so just do the best you can. The following methods may be used:

▶ Observe participants.

▶ Look at situation boards and reporting forms.

▶ Look at any reports.

▶ Talk with participants.

▶ Be a "fly on the wall" to listen into conversations and informal briefings.

Exercise objectives

1. Assess the ability of the communications team to develop the <<company name>> message, and produce the following communication materials: student, parent and employee communications via ENS, press releases, and community notifications.
2. Assess the effectiveness of the ENS and its use during the exercise.
3. Assess the ability of the Incident Commander to brief Executive Leadership Team.
4. Assess the ability of the Incident Commander (IC), and designated Team Leaders to conduct a timely Incident Action Planning meeting and develop a written IAP.
5. Incorporate the Satellite Operations Centers (SOC) into the exercise, and assess communications between the SOCs and the EOC. Determine gaps or overlaps, and note areas for improvement.

Exercise metrics

The above objectives will be evaluated on feedback using three methodologies: the debrief sessions, written evaluations, and observations by the observer and facilitator in the exercise environment.

Please return your written comments (please print if at all possible) to the exercise facilitator at the end of the exercise or type into the body of an email and return to <<email address>> in the next two days.

EVALUATION FORM

Based on feedback in debrief sessions, written evaluations & observations

JOBS WELL DONE	AREAS FOR IMPROVEMENT

Executive briefing document

Section 1: Your role as executive in this exercise

▶ Your task is to play your "usual executive role" by asking pertinent questions on how this situation is impacting partners, regions and the ability of team to continue to operate the business.

   ▷ We ask that you stay in role, play this situation as if it is really happening. You are there to receive a briefing on the current status of this significant and on-going event.

▶ If you plan to physically come to the EOC, when you arrive, please stay in role – if you are not in role, that will take the team members right out of theirs! We will group you together and guide you to the area where the briefing will occur.

   ▷ Your appearance at the EOC will be a great boost to the team so if it is possible for you to physically be there, it would be great!

▶ If you cannot attend and will call into the Executive Emergency conference bridge line, the Incident Commander will greet you and conduct an update briefing with your team.

▶ Please remember that the team will have been working through this exercise scenario since 9:00 this morning.

   ▷ If this were a real event, since this is an on-going event, this would not be your first briefing. In a real event you would, of course, have had several briefings prior to this call.

Section 2: The narrative

Include the information in the exercise plan, starting from "Exercise Type and Scope," and continuing through the narrative. Review the Artificialities, Assumptions, and Narrative for any timing changes that may be necessary due to the executive joining at the end of the exercise. (For example, instead of saying, "It is now 9:00 AM and the Incident Management team is about to meet," you would say, "The Incident Management team met at 9:00 AM.")

Section 3: Key issues

▶ Inability to occupy headquarters building for an unknown period of time.

▶ Trauma to employees.

▶ Reputational impact.

▶ Extensive media coverage of event.

▶ Potential decrease in stock price.

Functional exercise timing guideline

The following is a guideline on how to conduct a Functional exercise using the materials included in this chapter. The agenda assumes the exercise runs from 8:00 AM to 1:30 PM.

FUNCTIONAL EXERCISE TIMING GUIDELINE	
EXERCISE ACTIVITY – GUIDELINE	**TIME**
▶ Introductions (if necessary) ▶ Introduce exercise and how it will work ▶ Review exercise plan	8:00 AM – 8:25 AM
▶ Play radio broadcast	8:25 AM – 8:30 AM
▶ Exercise play 　> Deliver Sim Team calls from 9:45 – 11:30	8:30 AM – 11:45 AM
▶ Executive Briefing 　> Check speakerphone at least 30 minutes before the call.	11:45 AM – 12:10 PM
▶ Press Conference 　> Set up podium for press conference. 　> Review questions before the press conference to ensure they are appropriate.	12:10 PM – 12:30 PM
Debrief over lunch ▶ Ask players to grab lunch and get seated (a box lunch will help this go a bit faster) ▶ Debrief 　> What worked? 　> What needs improvement?	12:30 PM – 1:20 PM
Next steps	1:20 PM – 1:30 PM

Summary

A Functional exercise will provide your team with a realistic experience and valuable tool for improving their individual performance, their plans, and the company's overall emergency management program. Although these exercises are more time-intensive and expensive to produce than a Tabletop, the rewards are rich, and the experience is fulfilling for all who participate.

CHAPTER 15

Preparing the after-action report and exercise follow-up

Follow-up

Now that you have done all of that great work in designing the exercise, and have lived through the experience of delivering the exercise, you need to shift gears. Your next task is to develop the report that tells the story of the experience, captures the key learnings, and inspires people to take action. Your next task is to write the After-Action Report (AAR).

What is an AAR?

The After-Action Report, or AAR, is a formal record of the exercise and is where you provide a complete summary of the experience. The AAR serves several important functions. The AAR is where you will:

- ▶ Document response activities.
- ▶ Identify problems and successes.
- ▶ Assess plans and programs.
- ▶ Develop a plan of action.

Document response activities

The AAR is the best tool you have for detailing what was actually exercised. This includes the:

- ▶ Narrative.
- ▶ Players and departments.
- ▶ Plans and processes.

The AAR is the complete record of the exercise, which can be helpful for anyone who wants to know and understand how you exercise your plans. Many entities are interested in this report, for example the corporate audit risk committee, the risk department, your internal and external auditors, regulators, senior management, and/or the Board of Directors.

Identify problems/successes

The AAR is the best place to document problems and successes identified during the response and recovery operations. Remember, one of the reasons exercises are done is to find out the things that don't work – and once those are identified, plot a course of corrective action. These findings need to be carefully articulated so that a plan may be developed.

Assess plans and programs

The AAR is a great place to analyze the effectiveness of the exercised components of the plans, as well as the overall program. Every time you exercise a plan, you are assessing how it may perform in a "real event." The only way we know if any of the plans we write will work are to either conduct an exercise or have a disaster! Which would you prefer?

Develop a plan of action

The AAR is where a plan of action for implementing improvements can be described and defined. Once an issue that needs improvement has been identified, make recommendations for those improvements and suggest timelines and strategies to achieve the result.

Getting ready to write the report

Raw material

You will need a lot of material to write the report. It's important to know what you need ahead of time so you can remember what to save after the exercise. It is also very helpful to have a sense of how to receive the materials and organize them in a way that makes writing the report a bit easier. As you can see from the long list below, there will be a lot of information (and possibly paper as well)! Begin by reviewing all documentation from the exercise, including:

▶ Your facilitator notes.
▶ All of the Controller / Evaluator / Observer forms.

▶ Player evaluations.

▶ Simulation Team evaluations.

▶ Debriefing notes. (If you had two scribes, you will have a better chance of getting all the comments – but that also means you have to sift through two sets of notes).

▶ Any materials prepared by the participants that are tied to objectives:

   ▷ Communications.

   ▷ Incident Action Plans.

   ▷ Executive briefings.

   ▷ Completed Message Center forms.

   ▷ Status board/flip charts sheets.

   ▷ Photos.

Before you begin

Okay, so you remembered to gather all the materials listed above. They're now surrounding you at your desk after the exercise, so now you're going to start writing, right? Well, I find it helpful to take a day or two to reflect on the exercise experience before I start writing. Let it "roll around in your head" a bit. Even if the report needs to be written quickly, I find that a day or two of reflection always pays off. It gives me the chance to get a bit of distance and look across the experience as a whole. I often refer to this process of reflection as "mulching," a bit of passive review, as I'm not actively thinking about the exercise. It's just percolating in the deep recesses of my mind – like seeds germinating.

After a day or two, a little sprout of cohesiveness pops up and then I move to the next step of the process, which is what I call "noodling" where I put the exercise into the forefront of my brain and actively think about it, the overall experience, and the report I'm about to write. This is a great time to return to that basic question, *Why are we doing this exercise?* At this point in the process, the answer to the question this time will:

▶ Lead the direction and flow of the AAR.

▶ Keep you from going into areas that may not be applicable for this report.

Provide an overall 'guiding light' for the development of the report.

Report components

The report itself has two main components: the main body of the document, and the appendixes. The main body includes three basic chapters:

1. Executive summary.
2. Recommendations.
3. Facilitator's observations.

The appendix includes everything else:

▶ Debriefing summary.
▶ Controller / Evaluator / Observer comments.
▶ Evaluations:
   ▷ Participant.
   ▷ Simulation Team.
▶ Attendance and participant lists:
   ▷ Player lists.
   ▷ Exercise team.
   ▷ Design team.
   ▷ Simulation Team.
▶ Any specialized reports or information addendums. This could include copies of the Incident Action Plan (IAP), communications developed by a Communications Team, or written employee instructions.
▶ The exercise plan.
▶ Exercise images.

Main body – Executive summary

The Executive Summary is a short section found in the first page or two of the document that recaps the longer report. As the report is distributed to its many recipients, this summary may also be shored off as a separate, short document. As a stand-alone document, this section can be an ideal recap for a meeting, audit committee, or Board report. The summary allows the reader to rapidly become familiar with the larger body of material without having to read all the detail.

The Executive Summary usually contains a brief statement of the exercise goals, concise analysis of the exercise itself, and a summary of the main recommendations. One of the goals of the Executive Summary is to aid decision-making of busy business executives and managers who are less likely to dig into the remainder of the report.

Main body – Recommendations

Many people are immediately drawn to this section, often with hope tinged with a bit of anxiety. Recommendations generally draw from four key areas:

▶ Exercise objectives.
▶ Best practices.
▶ National standards.
▶ Benchmarking within the industry.

Exercise objectives

This continues to further point out the importance of well-written objectives. You will use the objectives as a baseline to evaluate the exercise, and you will likely comment on observations and areas for improvement within those objectives.

Best practices

If there are best practices in the field of emergency management or continuity planning that can be used as a tool to improve the program or plan under review, point them out. Guide the reader towards considerations on how to incorporate the best practice into future exercises and processes.=

National standards

The three standards that are most likely to be quoted in your AAR were recently adopted for the voluntary Private Sector Preparedness Accreditation and Certification Program (PS-Prep) by the Department of Homeland Security. PS-Prep is a partnership between DHS and the private sector that enables private entities to receive emergency preparedness certification from a DHS accreditation system, created in coordination with the private sector. Standards can help you frame the basis for your AAR, much like best practices.

The three standards that have been adopted are:

▶ **ASIS SPC.1-2009 Organizational Resilience**: Security Preparedness, and Continuity Management Systems. The American Society for Industrial Security (ASIS) has made ASIS SPC 1-2009 available for inspection, downloading, and printing at no cost.

  ▷ **http://www.asisonline.org/guidelines/ASIS SPC.1-2009 Item No. 1842.pdf**

▶ **British Standard 25999-2: 2007:** Business Continuity Management. The British Standards Institution (BSI) has made BS25999 available for inspection, downloading, and printing for a nominal charge.

  ▷ **http://www.bsiamerica.com/en-us/Assessment-and-Certification-services/Management-systems/Standards-and-schemes/BS-25999/**

▶ **National Fire Protection Association 1600: 2007:** Standard on Disaster/Emergency Management and Business Continuity Programs. The National Fire Protection Association (NFPA) is making NFPA 1600 available for inspection, downloading, and printing at no cost.

  ▷ **http://www.nfpa.org/assets/files/PDF/NFPA1600.pdf**

Benchmarking within the industry

There may be key indicators within your industry that can be used to evaluate performance; if so, it is useful to use them for comparison. You might find these in:

▶ Published documents and journals.
▶ Articles from professional organizations and societies.
▶ National studies or white papers.
▶ Professional association websites.

Recommendation side-bar #1: Framing the recommendations

Recommendations are always best received when they are straightforward, fact-based, and tied to practices or standards. Because many people focus exclusively on this section, it can, therefore, be littered with political "landmines." You will always need to keep this in mind when writing the recommendations. You want people to hear what you have to say, but if all of their walls are up in defense, it is harder for them to do that. Whenever possible, footnote (or otherwise reference) practices or standards in your recommendation as it will help build support and place weight behind them.

As you are writing the recommendations, it is always good to remember that basic question, *Why are we doing this exercise?* As you are mulling that over, there are two other questions to ask yourself:

▶ What do you want these recommendations to do?

▶ Who is the audience for the report?

These two questions will also be helpful in developing the tone and style of the report.

The "average" number of recommendations in an AAR obviously varies by many factors, including experience level of the team, length of time of exercise, quality of the plans, and number of players. There can often be quite a few; anywhere from 10 to 20 recommendations would probably be considered 'average.' In general, though, I would avoid doing over 20 recommendations. That many would likely overwhelm the readers and give them a sense of anxiety: with so much work to be done, where do they start? If you find yourself with 20, 25, 30 recommendations, I suggest reviewing the whole set, focus on the most urgent issues, then work on other items over time.

When writing each recommendation, as when writing exercise goals, start each with an action-oriented verb for clarity. Use verbs such as "describe," "implement," "incorporate," "assess," "conduct," "perform," or "initiate." Then go on to describe a clearly stated required action.

Sample recommendations

▶ "Incorporate Incident Action Planning (IAP) into Incident Management Team (IMT) processes. As practiced in the exercise, the IAP process is one of the hallmarks of effective emergency management. This simple planning tool allows teams to organize around agreed-upon objectives and a set time to meet again."

▶ "Develop FAQs for managers on pandemic plan implementation. Managers tasked with implementing the pandemic plan need guidance on basic issues that will surface. These include fundamental Human Resources issues, such as managing sick staff. To provide consistent guidance, start a simple FAQ document that can grow as issues arise and evolve."

Recommendation side-bar #2: Semantics

Words can carry a lot of weight, and in some organizations or industries, they carry more weight than others. In particular, I offer some words of caution about the word "recommendation." We have had several clients over the past few years that have asked us to change the word "recommendation" to another word, less loaded with 'baggage.'

Some clients have been targeted in their regulatory audits because they had elected not to embrace an exercise "recommendation." They found they were being judged on something that was not a national standard, but which had been "recommended" to them. In the audit world, the word "recommendation" can be very significant and often means that the company or department is required to take the recommended action. To that end, for some clients, we now use the word "observations" rather than "recommendations."

Main Body – Facilitator observations

There are many things that the Facilitator will see and observe during the exercise. It is important to capture these observations and share them. What do you report on and what do you not? There are a couple drivers to decide what you report on and what you do not. Some considerations:

▶ The answer to the basic question, *Why are we doing this exercise?*
▶ The exercise objectives – what you are observing against the objectives.

When writing observations, they must be:

▶ Fact-based.
▶ Clear.

▶ Concise.

▶ Tied back to standards, practices, and industry benchmarking when possible.

Keep in mind that even if the team has made a *zillion* mistakes, the tone and the framing of the observations can still be positive and encouraging. I always like to remind readers and players that it is always better to have made these mistakes in an exercise (with the implied chance of correcting them) than to make them during a real disaster.

Appendix – Debriefing comments

This section should detail the results of the debriefing session. Preface the section by detailing what questions were asked. We always ask just two simple questions of the exercise players, "What worked?" and "What didn't work?" (or "What needed improvement?").

Be sure to edit the comments sufficiently so that they make sense and have a flow to them; however, don't edit them so much that you take out the meaning or context. Lastly, if you have asked particular groups to make comments, call out those groups by name either within the body of the comment, or as a separate group section. For example, "The *Operations Team* noted that security must be added outside the EOC to check badges and keep non-authorized people out."

Appendix – Evaluator / Controller / Observer comments

Organize the evaluator / controller / observer names into a table like the one below, noting the teams they were assigned to observe.

TEAM	EVALUATOR
Command	R. Jones
Operations	T. Smith
Planning & Intelligence	G. Williams
Logistics	D. Johnson
Finance	E. Wilson

Under the table, note the comments by team or function title, and list the observations under the two questions, "What worked?" and "What didn't work" (or "What needs improvement?").

Observer comments are usually included in the AAR verbatim – with the following exception: If the comment is based on a personal issue or the tone is inappropriate, it may be edited, or even deleted. Some valid observations are best delivered in person rather than in writing. It is one thing to share an observation verbally and quite another to see it on a page in black and white.

Appendix – Exercise plan

In this appendix, include the entire exercise plan. This provides a great background for the AAR, and is a historical record of what you actually did in the exercise. It also helps put everything into context for readers of the AAR who may not have been in attendance. It's not usually necessary to include injects in the AAR, but be sure to save them – they come in very handy for future exercises.

Appendix – Evaluations

Participant evaluations

It is often useful to be able to see exactly how the participants felt about the exercise by including the evaluations into the AAR. However, transcribing the participant evaluations can take a lot of time, especially for a large exercise. As mentioned in Chapter 9, an electronic survey (such as Survey Monkey or Zoomerang) may speed up the process; however, the return rate is often quite a bit lower. As with Controller / Evaluator / Observer comments, participant evaluation comments are usually presented verbatim with the same caveat – if a comment is based on a personal issue or the tone is inappropriate, it may be edited or even deleted.

Simulation Team evaluations

Simulation Team evaluations should include questions specifically focused on exercise design and delivery. Just as with the other evaluation comments, the responses to the questions should be presented verbatim, with the same caveat.

Appendix – Special documents and reports

Other documents or reports that you might want to add into the AAR include Incident Action Plans (IAPs), and any communications that have been issued (such as press releases, employee and client messages, social media releases, or website updates). Any deliverable that was part of the exercise objectives are ideal to include in this section.

Appendix – Attendance lists

Some organizations may need or want to have a permanent record of who actually attended the exercise. This can help to satisfy audit requirements; in some organizations it provides an additional incentive to attend. As part of the formal record, you might also wish to keep a roster of who was on the exercise Design Team and Simulation Team as well.

Appendix – Exercise images

Taking photos during an exercise provides an excellent record of the event, as well as being another tool to promote the activity and the overall program. Most participants enjoy seeing them; they can be used in company newsletters or websites promoting the overall program. They also provide a nice touch on the AAR cover page and within the report. Photographs can also be shared directly with participants and departments.

Report editing

Once the report is complete, have at least one other person read it. You are too close to it to catch errors, and you don't want to send it out without another set of eyes poring over the context, grammar, spelling, and flow. If you are blessed to have someone in your group with good writing and editing skills, ask them to look it over. Just keep in mind that you shouldn't take suggestions or revisions personally; it's all about getting the best document and, therefore, the best results.

Report follow-up

Once the report is written, edited, and ready to be sent, you may be thinking that you can take a deep breath and sigh as you sink into a cozy chair. Done – finally!

Alas, you're not done yet, not by a long shot! Like everything in the field of emergency management, you are really never done. (Sorry to be the bearer of that news.) Here's your short list of what you should be thinking about now:

- ▶ Getting the report in front of the right people.
- ▶ Gain consensus on a plan of action:
    - ▷ Plan revisions.
    - ▷ Assignments.
    - ▷ Required funding.
- ▶ Tracking and follow-up.
- ▶ Scheduling the next exercise.

Getting the report in front of the right people

This is an important step. Acceptance of the report and recommendations by key individuals is likely to be tied to funding and other key resources. You need to find how who "right people" are. Here is a partial list to consider when "shopping" your report around:

- ▶ Your corporate sponsor.
- ▶ Corporate Risk Committee.
- ▶ Senior management.
- ▶ Senior audit management.

In many cases, getting the AAR in front of the "right people" is simply a matter of sending it to them – after all, everyone has email these days, even executives. However, getting them to read it requires a little more thought. It is always good to consider what the hook is for them – what speaks to them in particular? They may pay more attention to the report if you can tie the recommendations to:

- ▶ Company audit results.
- ▶ Key company initiatives.
- ▶ Areas that you know will "strike a chord" with key management.

Do your research and find out a key player's particular interest. Some gentle words of caution, though: This might be a political quagmire in your organization. Tread lightly and be observant at all times.

Gain consensus on a plan of action

Before you can develop a plan of action, ensure that those responsible for, and charged with, fixing the issues understands them. Educate those players about the recommendations and appropriate standards. Chart a course of action that will result in the successful resolution of the recommendations. As part of this plan, you will need to develop the strategy for:

▶ Plan revisions.

▶ Assignments.

▶ Required funding.

Tracking and follow-up

Once you have an agreed upon plan of action, take time to chart all recommendations and action steps, including a timeline for completion. All deliverables need an owner and a completion date; some may also include intermediate dates as "touch points." Don't forget to consider whether you have the resources that you need to achieve the recommendation. This includes people, applications, equipment, and other items. If you discover you have a shortfall, determine the possible work-arounds to build success.

Tracking tools

Tracking tools are important to chart progress towards achievement of the goals and program improvement. They could be a simple Excel spreadsheet or could be something more complex, like a project management software application. (I must confess that I am a big fan for the concept of "the simpler the better"!) How you track the work is up to you. The critically important thing is to follow up – follow-up is the key!

A tracking sheet doesn't have to be extensive; a simple format would include the following information:

▶ Category or area to work on.

▶ Task.

▶ Responsible party.

▶ Due date.

▶ Status.

▶ Comments.

This step is absolutely essential to ensure that actions are completed. There is nothing more disappointing to come around to the next exercise and discover that very few of the identified initiatives were completed from the last exercise. Over time, this is demoralizing to you and to the team. The best BCP mangers are those who have figured out how to get things done; the way they do that is to walk the *very fine line* between being a cheerleader and being a nag!

Scheduling the next exercise

How do you know if your improvements made a difference and your revised plan is better than the last one? Of course, you already know the answer to this simple, rhetorical question! Either have a disaster and see how it goes or do another exercise! And as you already know, the latter is less stressful and generally bears the best results!

Summary

There is tremendous power in conducting exercises, but their value is limited if there is no documentation that they ever happened, or what could be done to better them. An After-Action Report provides key feedback to everyone involved.

We have now come full circle in the process of exercise design. As you can see, it begins and ends with an exercise. Exercises remain one of your most powerful tools to improve your program, your plan, and your people.

CHAPTER 16

Developing an annual or multi-year exercise and training calendar

Do you have an exercise or training calendar in your organization? In my experience, most entities don't. For some, holding an exercise is almost an afterthought, as in, "Oh my! We need to do an exercise before year-end!" For others, an exercise becomes a priority after an audit finding notes the absence of an annual exercise. And still others may know they have to conduct an exercise and have a general idea of when they might want to hold it – but they put off actually scheduling it until it becomes a "hurry up!" situation.

The goal of this chapter is to encourage you to develop an annual calendar or – better yet – a multi-year calendar for exercises and training. What would be the advantages and benefits of this type of forward thinking? I'll explore what an annual calendar might look like a little later, but first, let's explore the Federal Emergency Management Agency's (FEMA) HSEEP program.

Raising the bar

The FEMA Homeland Security Exercise and Evaluation Program ("HSEEP" as it is known in the alphabet soup world of federal programs) is raising the bar on exercise planning. FEMA describes HSEEP as a "capabilities and performance-based exercise program that provides a standardized methodology and terminology for exercise design, development, conduct, evaluation, and improvement planning." [12] What a mouthful!

I applaud many of HSEEP's processes and its efforts towards standardization. I also think one of its greatest contributions is the idea of planning for multiple years, and wrapping that planning around the organization's goals and established priorities.

HSEEP requires agencies to develop a "multi-year training and exercise plan," which is described as a "foundational document for guiding a successful exercise program." One of the key aspects of this document is that it ties training and exercise activities toward an organization's preparedness goals. What a concept! It utilizes a building block approach for training and exercise activities, then uses graphs and matrices to illustrate training and exercise activities that support the identified priorities.

As training and exercises are completed, the document can be updated annually (at a minimum), modified, and revised to reflect changes to the priorities and new capabilities that need to be assessed. Sounds like a pretty smart approach to achieving program goals.

Building your calendar

When getting started crafting your program (and, therefore, building your own training and exercise schedule), there are two main underlying themes to remember:

1. Think in terms of a building block approach.
2. Tie activities to the program goals.

Building block approach

This concept was discussed when we reviewed the exercise types in Chapter 2. Effective team development is based on a series of building blocks, starting with providing training and workshops (often combined with Orientation exercises) and then continuing to challenge the team until they have reached their appropriate competency level.

Once you have established the basic skill set, your bi-annual exercise activity becomes a deepening of the skills at that exercise-type level. This logical progression of exercises helps to build capabil-

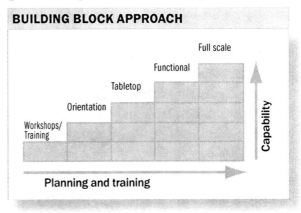

ities and competence.

When starting out conducting exercises, we know that we begin with an Orientation exercise and work our way "up" (in complexity) from there. Many organizations will reach their appropriate competency level at a Tabletop exercise; some will advance to a Functional exercise. (With the exception of public-sector entities, the overly ambitious, or those with field response requirements, few organizations advance to a Full-scale exercise.)

Tie activities to program goals

Do you have goals for your emergency management program? Are those goals for one year? Multiple years? What would it look like if you plotted those goals out over time and tied the goals to training and exercises for the appropriate groups? For this discussion, we'll take a look at the XYZ Company. As Rod Sterling used to say on the Twilight Zone, "Imagine if you will..."

Company XYZ has the following Emergency Management Program goals for the next three calendar years:

1. Implement the Incident Command System at the company headquarters, roll out to all locations nationwide within three years. **(Goal 1)**
2. Improve both internal and external communication by creating a crisis communications plan and communication templates, and holding regular exercises of the communications team. **(Goal 2)**
3. Install a company-wide notification system, deploy to the entire company over a period of three years. **(Goal 3)**
4. Assess the accuracy and viability of mission-critical department business continuity plans (BCP) and validate the recovery time objectives (RTO). **(Goal 4)**
5. Assess the capabilities of the technology Disaster Recovery Plan (DRP), and cross-validate the recovery time objectives (RTO) with the departments' BCPs. **(Goal 5)**
6. Develop Incident Management Teams in regional office locations in the United States through a series of trainings and tabletop exercises. **(Goal 6)**

The Emergency Management Program manager is pretty clear on her program goals (above). Next, she has plotted out the activities over a three-year period. When doing this, she took into account the corporate calendar, any "sensitive" business times of the year, and holiday schedules. Her multi-year exercise schedule might look like the charts on the next 3 pages.

Develop a project plan or task list

Since our fictional manager now knows what she wants her calendar to look like for the next 3 years, her next step is to break down the calendar into "bite-sized" chunks, by developing a project plan or a task list.

Whether your organization has a dedicated PMO (Project Management Office) you can tap into, or whether you need (or want) to do it yourself, review the timing of each event on the calendar and start working backwards in identifying what needs to be done. For exercises, you can use the sample timelines for Orientation, Tabletop, and Functional exercises in Chapters 12, 13, and 14, respectively, to start plotting your time and tasks. For other events, create something similar so you'll know what to do and when to do it.

"Shop it around"

Once she has completed the matrix, XYZ's Emergency Response Program manager can see what's happening in each year and quarter, and draft a budget to complete each annual cycle. At that point, she can circulate it to the program sponsors to gather their support and funding.

Obviously, getting management support and budget will vary from company to company, but plotting the program over multiple years makes it easier to see what needs to be done, and therefore, easier to develop an appropriate budget. For our fictional manager, once she has gotten the funding and support (both are needed!), she is ready to send the three-year training and exercise calendar out to the participants.

Benefits

There are many benefits to a multi-year program calendar. Those planning benefits include:

1. Helps the organization to allocate limited resources such as materials,

MULTIYEAR EXERCISE SCHEDULE: YEAR ONE

ENTITY	Qtr 1			Qtr 2			Qtr 3			Qtr 4		
	J	F	M	A	M	J	J	A	S	O	N	D
EXECUTIVE MGMT TEAM (EMT)							Work-shop GOAL 1		IMT Exercise GOAL 1			
INCIDENT MGMT TEAM (IMT)	HQ ICS Orientation GOAL 1	ENS Roll out GOAL 3	ENS Exercise GOAL 3	Com Workshop GOAL 2	HQ ICS Tabletop GOAL 1		ENS Exercise GOAL 3	Com Exercise GOAL 2	HQ ICS Functional GOAL 1		ENS Exercise GOAL 3	Com Exercise GOAL 2
IT / DR				DR Orientation Exercise GOAL 5						DR Tabletop Exercise GOAL 5		
MISSION CRITICAL DEPTS.						BCP Orientation GOAL 4					BCP Tabletop GOAL 4	
SATELLITE LOCATIONS						Orientation GOAL 6			Tabletop Group 1 GOAL 6			Tabletop Group 2 GOAL 6

GOAL 1/ ICS implementation GOAL 2 / Communications GOAL 3/ ENS system GOAL 4/ BCP GOAL 5/ DR GOAL 6/ Satellite locations

MULTIYEAR EXERCISE SCHEDULE: YEAR TWO

ENTITY	Qtr 1			Qtr 2			Qtr 3			Qtr 4		
	J	F	M	A	M	J	J	A	S	O	N	D
EXECUTIVE MGMT TEAM (EMT)			Participate in functional GOAL 1						Participate in functional GOAL 1			
INCIDENT MGMT TEAM (IMT)		EMS exercise GOAL 3	HQ functional GOAL 1	Com exercise GOAL 2				EMS exercise GOAL 3	HQ functional GOAL 1	Com exercise GOAL 2		
IT / DR				DR hotsite exercise GOAL 5						DR hotsite exercise GOAL 5		
MISSION CRITICAL DEPTS.					BCP tabletop GOAL 4						BCP tabletop GOAL 4	
SATELLITE LOCATIONS				Tabletop Group 1 GOAL 6	Tabletop Group 2 GOAL 6						Tabletop Group 1 GOAL 6	Tabletop Group 2 GOAL 6

GOAL 1/ ICS implementation   GOAL 2 / Communications   GOAL 3/ ENS system   GOAL 4/ BCP   GOAL 5/ DR   GOAL 6/ Satellite locations

MULTIYEAR EXERCISE SCHEDULE: YEAR THREE

ENTITY	Qtr 1			Qtr 2			Qtr 3			Qtr 4		
	J	F	M	A	M	J	J	A	S	O	N	D
EXECUTIVE MGMT TEAM (EMT)			Participate in functional GOAL 1						Participate in functional GOAL 1			
INCIDENT MGMT TEAM (IMT)	ICS training west coast GOAL 1	EMS exercise GOAL 3	HQ functional GOAL 1	Com exercise GOAL 2		ICS training east coast GOAL 1		EMS exercise GOAL 3	HQ functional GOAL 1	Com exercise GOAL 2	ICS training midwest GOAL 1	
IT / DR				DR hotsite exercise GOAL 5						DR hotsite exercise GOAL 5		
MISSION CRITICAL DEPTS.					BCP tabletop GOAL 4						BCP tabletop GOAL 4	
SATELLITE LOCATIONS				Tabletop Group 1 GOAL 6	Tabletop Group 2 GOAL 6						Tabletop Group 1 GOAL 6	Tabletop Group 2 GOAL 6

GOAL 1 / ICS implementation   GOAL 2 / Communications   GOAL 3 / ENS system   GOAL 4 / BCP   GOAL 5 / DR   GOAL 6 / Satellite locations staff, and time in an orderly and systematic manner.

2. Assists decision makers by providing guidelines and goals for future actions.

3. Facilitates communication among all of the participants within the organization, both horizontally and vertically.

4. Helps the BCP manager employ more control in developing the program, establish goals "proactively," and consider contingencies.

5. Insures that a consistent set of actions is implemented across the company, and that those actions are coherent with the values and priorities of the organization.

6. Helps to quantify program goals and establish a method of measuring success.

7. Avoids "scope creep" of the program goals.

And the greatest benefit of all is that everyone knows what is going on and what is expected of them. With clear program goals, a detailed calendar, and a specific project plan or task list, there should be no confusion about who is to do what when.

Summary

There are many great benefits in developing a multi-year training and exercise calendar. This requires you to develop clear goals for the program, and then to plot them out over time. The greatest benefit is that everyone knows what is going on and what is expected of them. To build a successful program, you need people who are actively engaged and supporting your efforts every step of the way.

CHAPTER 17

Exercise design resource list

There are a variety of places to look for ideas and resource information on exercise design. The purpose of this chapter is to give you an idea of where to look and point you in that direction.

Federal Emergency Management Agency (FEMA)

FEMA's mission is to support our citizens and first responders to ensure that as a nation we work together to build, sustain, and improve our capability to prepare for, protect against, respond to, recover from, and mitigate all hazards [13].

The Federal Emergency Management Agency (FEMA) has long been a resource for materials and ideas on how to conduct exercises (www.fema.gov). A good place to begin is to simply go to the FEMA website and do a search on "exercises."

FEMA Independent Study

FEMA provides the nation and the world with an incredible training library that is both free and "always on." The Independent Study Program is a treasure trove of information. There are several modules on exercise design. As of this printing, these were these current offerings:

IS-120.a An introduction to exercises

IS 120.a introduces the basics of emergency management exercises. It also builds a foundation for subsequent exercise courses, which provide the specifics of the Homeland Security Exercise and Evaluation Program (HSEEP) and

---

13 http://www.fema.gov/about/index.shtm

the National Standard Exercise Curriculum (NSEC).
  http://www.training.fema.gov/EMIWeb/IS/IS120A.asp

IS-130 Exercise evaluation and improvement planning
IS 130 introduces the basics of emergency management exercise evaluation and improvement planning. It also builds a foundation for exercise evaluation concepts as identified in the Homeland Security Exercise and Evaluation Program (HSEEP).
  http://www.training.fema.gov/EMIWeb/IS/IS130.asp

IS/G 139: Exercise design course (continuity of operations)
The Exercise Design Course (IS/B139) provides continuity managers with the exercise development and planning skills for designing and conducting continuity exercises. This course is also offered in a web-based version. The course's primary learning objectives are to introduce the fundamentals of tabletop, functional and full-scale exercise design, and address the importance of conducting exercises and components of a comprehensive and progressive exercise program.
  http://www.training.fema.gov/EMIWeb/IS/is139.asp

FEMA Homeland Security Exercise and Evaluation Program (HSEEP)
The Federal Emergency Management Agency (FEMA) National Exercise Division (NED) manages HSEEP to promote consistency among exercises across the nation as a means to enhance national preparedness. HSEEP is a capabilities- and performance-based exercise program that provides a standardized guidance and terminology for exercise design, development, conduct, evaluation, and improvement planning. A key component of HSEEP is fostering self-sustaining exercise programs by providing jurisdictions with consistent doctrine and resources for program management.

City, County, and State Office of Emergency Services
These offices might be called a variety of different things in your area or state:

▶ Emergency Management Agency (EMA).

▶ Office of Emergency Services (OES).

▶ Homeland Security and Emergency Management.

These agencies are all tasked with conducting exercises and will often host training programs as well. Contact your local agency and speak to the local exercise specialist and see if you can attend an exercise, perhaps be an observer or attend a training.

California Specialized Training Institute (CSTI)

California has a great state training program. The California Specialized Training Institute (CSTI) is a gem, providing low-cost training in many different disciplines. CSTI offers many other specialized seminars, customized courses, and/or grant-funded courses. Information about their training opportunities can be found at www.csti.ca.gov.

Local business continuity and emergency management groups

Local business continuity and emergency management groups are another resource. These groups may offer workshops or trainings, however, their greatest assistance might be in the area of networking. These groups are great places to meet other professionals who might be doing an exercise in the future and allow outside observers to participate. Many people need another set of hands during an exercise and that could be you! This is a great learning opportunity for you, while you also provide valuable feedback to your colleague as an outside set of eyes and ears.

National training conferences and conventions

This is a great place to find formal training and informal networking with peers and colleagues. Many of these groups also sponsor a professional publication as well. The better known conferences include:

▶ The Disaster Recovery Journal – www.drj.com

▶ World Conference on Disaster Management – www.wcdm.org

▶ Continuity and Planning Management – www.contingencyplanning.com

▶ Continuity Insights - www.continuityinsights.com

Audio-visual resources

A professionally produced audio-visual radio broadcast or "news video" clip can really make your exercise explode with realism and excitement! We have used a great voice-over artist and recording genius for the past ten years. Scott Keck, founder of "Local Fool," an AV company based in San Francisco, does an incredible job for us. He produces all of the materials and then delivers them to me anywhere in the world as .mp3 or .mov files. You can find Scott at improviz@comcast.net.

Summary

The advice we give to our exercise players – practice, practice and more practice – applies to designing exercises, too. To become good at what you do and skilled in your design process, you simply need to practice, practice, practice: design, participate, and observe a lot of exercises. With enough training and practice, it may even become intuitive. Always be on the look-out for training and participation opportunities.

Glossary

▶ **AFTER-ACTION REPORT (AAR)** – A summary of lessons learned from an exercise or an incident. The AAR also includes recommendations for improvements.

▶ **BUSINESS CONTINUITY EXERCISE** – An exercise that tests the recovery of a mission-critical business process or business department.

▶ **BUSINESS CONTINUITY PLANS (BCP)** – The creation and validation of a practiced plan for how an entity (for profit, not-for-profit or government) will recover and restore partially or completely interrupted critical business functions within a predetermined time after an incident or extended disruption.

▶ **CONTROLLERS** – Person who, during an exercise, maintains order and helps to facilitate the exercise proceeding according to plan. May also act as an evaluator. Used primarily in large functional and full-scale exercises.

▶ **CRISIS COMMUNICATIONS** – Communications response to a crisis (incident, event), focusing on factual communication by an involved organization to its stakeholders and the public.

▶ **CRISIS MANAGEMENT TEAM** – See "Incident Management Team."

▶ **DISASTER RECOVERY EXERCISE** – An exercise that tests the disaster recovery or technology recovery aspects of a plan.

▶ **DRILL** – A supervised field response activity with a limited focus to test a particular procedure. Drills usually highlight and closely examine a limited portion of the overall emergency management plan.

▶ **DR EXERCISE** – See "Disaster Recovery exercise."

▶ **EMERGENCY INCIDENT** – An incident or occurrence that requires an immediate response to bring the situation under control and restore normality, and which can threaten the health or safety of those involved, responders, and people in the surrounding area.

▶ **EMERGENCY MANAGEMENT** – The organization and management of resources and responsibilities for dealing with all aspects of emergencies, including mitigation, preparedness, response and recovery.

▶ **EMERGENCY OPERATIONS CENTER (EOC)** – An established location/facility in which selected management can receive information pertaining to an incident and from which they can provide direction, coordination, and support to emergency operations.

▶ **EMERGENCY RESPONSE EXERCISE** – An exercise that tests the emergency response aspects of a plan.

▶ **EVALUATORS** – Person who, during an exercise, is assigned to teams or groups specifically to appraise the activities that they observe. The evaluation is made against the exercise objectives.

▶ **EXERCISE CONTROL TEAM** – Individuals who are responsible for exercise evaluation and oversight. This can include evaluators, controllers and observers. They all work under the direction of the Exercise Facilitator.

▶ **EXERCISE DESIGN TEAM** – A group of individuals who are tasked with assisting in the design of the exercise. These individuals are commonly subject matter experts from the organization. Their role includes validating the exercise narrative and developing the exercise injects.

▶ **EXERCISE FACILITATOR/DIRECTOR** – The individual in charge of the exercise from design through the delivery of the exercise. He or she may also be the author of the After Action Report.

▶ **EXERCISE INJECTS** – Information that is inserted or "injected" into the exercise that expands the story, provides information, asks a question and/or engages the exercise players to "do something."

▶ **EXERCISE PLAN** – The complete background of the exercise, including the narrative. The exercise plan provides all of the necessary background information for the players to begin the exercise. Also called the "player's book."

▶ **EXERCISE PLAYERS** – All participants in the exercise who are chartered with responding to the event.

▶ **EXERCISE SCRIPT** – The text of the Exercise Inject.

▶ **EXERCISE TEAM** – The entire team of individuals who are involved in the management of the exercise. This includes the exercise facilitator/director, exercise Design Team, Simulation team, Evaluator, Controller, and Observers.

▶ **FULL-SCALE EXERCISE** – An exercise which tests the mobilization of all or as many as possible of the response components, takes place in "real time," employs real equipment, and tests several emergency functions.

▶ **FUNCTIONAL EXERCISE** – An exercise which simulates a disaster in the most realistic manner possible without moving real people or equipment to a real site. A functional exercise utilizes a carefully designed and scripted scenario, with timed messages and communications between players and simulators.

▶ **GOAL** – A broad statement of the reason the exercise is being conducted. The goal explains what is being assessed or evaluated.

▶ **HOMELAND SECURITY EXERCISE AND EVALUATION PROGRAM (HSEEP)** – A capabilities and performance-based exercise program that provides a standardized methodology and terminology for exercise design, development, conduct, evaluation, and improvement planning.

▶ **INCIDENT ACTION PLAN (IAP)** – A document that contains objectives reflecting the overall incident strategy and specific tactical actions and supporting information for the next operational period on an incident.

▶ **INITIAL ASSESSMENT TEAM (IAT)** – Team responsible for evaluating incidents, assigning an incident level and determining if plans should be activated.

▶ **INCIDENT COMMAND SYSTEM (ICS)** – A systematic tool used for the command, control, and coordination of response and recovery operations. ICS allows organizations to work together using common terminology and operating procedures to control personnel, facilities, equipment, and communications at a single incident scene. It facilitates a consistent response to any incident by employing a common organizational structure that can be expanded and contracted in a logical manner based on the level of required response.

▶ **INCIDENT MANAGEMENT TEAM** – The tactical team in charge of managing an incident from response through recovery.

▶ **KEY INJECTS** – Designated injects that will be tracked from injection into the exercise through the successful management/conclusion. Key injects are tracked by evaluators and/or controllers in the exercise who work closely with the simulation team to ensure that the event is managed.

▶ **MASTER SCENARIO EVENTS LIST (MSEL)** – A chronologically sequenced outline of the simulated events and key event descriptions that participants will be asked to respond to during the course of exercise play.

▶ **MESSAGE CENTER** – Group of people who receives, records, and routes calls/information about resources reporting to the incident and resource status.

▶ **"MULCHING"** – The passive act of dropping an issue or idea into the back of the mind and allowing it to "roll around" until ideas come to the forefront.

▶ **NATIONAL INCIDENT MANAGEMENT SYSTEM (NIMS)** – A system mandated by Homeland Security Presidential Directive 5 that provides a consistent nationwide approach for governments, the private sector, and non-governmental organizations, to work effectively and efficiently together to prepare for, respond to, and recover from domestic incidents, regardless of cause, size, or complexity.

▶ **"NOODLING"** – Next step after "mulching." Once an idea sprouts, the thinker begins to actively think about the issue until ideas are developed.

▶ **OBJECTIVES** – The specific activities and deliverables that will be required in the exercise.

▶ **OBSERVERS** – Individuals assigned to monitor specific groups or teams. They are asked to record their observations. They report to the exercise facilitator or a controller/evaluator.

▶ **OPERATIONAL PERIOD** – The period of time scheduled for execution of a given set of operation actions as specified in the Incident Action Plan. Operational Periods can be of various lengths, although usually not over 24 hours.

▶ **ORIENTATION EXERCISE** – A basic exercise using a simple narrative and delivered in a PowerPoint slide format in a conversational, non-threatening manner. It is often used to orient a team to a plan or a plan to a team.

▶ **"PARKING LOT"** – A flip chart or whiteboard that will be used to capture any questions or issues that come up during the training but can't be addressed at that time. The usual practice is to revisit any "parking lot" issues at the end of the training and make a plan for addressing any unresolved questions or issues at that time.

▶ **PARTICIPANT INSTRUCTIONS** – Informs the exercise players what they can expect from the exercise and what is expected of them during the exercise.

▶ **PREPAREDNESS** – The wide range of deliberate, critical tasks and activities necessary to build, sustain, and improve the operational capability to prevent, protect against, respond to, and recover from domestic incidents.

▶ **"PLAYER'S BOOK"** – See "Exercise Plan."

▶ **TABLETOP, ADVANCED** – Same as a Basic Tabletop, with the addition of a Simulation Team present in the exercise room.

▶ **TABLETOP, BASIC** – An exercise using written and verbal scenarios to evaluate the effectiveness of an organization's emergency management plan and procedures and to highlight issues of coordination and assignment of responsibilities. Tabletop exercises do not physically simulate specific events, do not utilize equipment, and do not deploy resources.

▶ **"TEACHABLE MOMENTS"** – An unplanned opportunity that arises in the exercise where a facilitator/controller/evaluator has an ideal chance to offer insight to his or her players. It is a fleeting opportunity that must be sensed and seized.

CPSIA information can be obtained at www.ICGtesting.com
Printed in the USA
BVOW05s1335250314

348718BV00004B/13/P